A SEASON FOR COURAGE

Favorite Talks from
Especially for Youth

A SEASON FOR COURAGE

Favorite Talks from
Especially for Youth

Bookcraft
Salt Lake City, Utah

Library of Congress Catalog Card Number 99-72555
ISBN 1-57008-662-1

First Printing, 1999

Printed in the United States of America

Special appreciation is expressed to the contributors to this work for their willingness to share their thoughts and testimonies with youth. Each author accepts complete responsibility for the material contained within his or her chapter. There is no endorsement for this work (real or implied) by The Church of Jesus Christ of Latter-day Saints, the Church Educational System, or Brigham Young University.

CONTENTS

A Season for Courage

"Shall the youth of Zion falter in defending truth and right?
While the enemy assaileth, shall we shrink or shun the fight?
No!"

—HYMNS, NO. 254

Not long ago, I was waiting for a subway in New York City. As I stood among literally hundreds of other people, crowding and jostling, I could feel myself being inched ever closer toward the tracks. Suddenly, with vivid clarity, I recalled a true story that I had read in a magazine. Many years ago, a four-year-old girl was holding her mother's hand while waiting for a subway in New York. Similar to my experience—perhaps this is what jarred the memory—the growing crowd began to inch closer to the tracks. As the anxious crowd pushed forward, the young girl lost her grip of her mother's hand and fell onto the tracks. As I thought about this story, I peered onto the subway tracks and realized that this young girl had fallen four feet below the platform! People began to shout for someone to save the little girl lying on the tracks below, but nobody stepped forward.

To make matters worse, the lights of an oncoming train could be seen rapidly approaching. Finally, a man named Everett Sanderson, who was thirty-five feet away from the girl, jumped onto the tracks and raced towards her. Moments before the train reached the injured girl, Everett scooped her up and threw her into the arms of those standing on the platform above him. In desperation, he jumped towards the platform, where a policeman, the child's aunt, and another would-be rescuer joined together and lifted him from the tracks. The screeching train just missed Everett Sanderson's legs, brushing them as he was lifted to safety.

I stood looking at the tracks, almost hypnotized, as I reflected upon this story. I firmly stood my ground as I thought of the possibility of being accidentally pushed onto the tracks. But more importantly, I was amazed at the courage of Everett Sanderson and wondered if I, in the same circumstances, would have demonstrated similar courage.

Courage

Most people would define courage as "meeting danger without fear" or "bravery." With such a definition, it is of little wonder that courage is always linked with dramatic acts. Remember the cowardly lion in the classic *Wizard of Oz*? He, like most people, believed that courage came from doing something spectacular, from a display of extraordinary valor or conspicuous bravery. He sought courage as if courage were an award or some type of certificate that stated, "You are courageous." The cowardly lion received his medal in the end and was declared a hero. I have come to conclude that wearing a medal doesn't make anyone more courageous than wearing a Halloween costume makes someone an actual vampire. It is clear that real courage is not makeup, but what we are made of.

The original roots of *courage* mean "heart." Courage is not just about danger or even adventure but about acting in accordance with what is ultimately in one's heart. Let's return to Everett Sanderson, the subway rescuer. Some may think that I fell into a limiting definition of courage by using this dramatic tale to begin my story. But as with most experiences, there is more to this story. I believe Everett Sanderson was courageous not because he jumped onto subway tracks in front of a speeding train but because of something he said in an interview following the rescue: "If I hadn't tried to save that little girl, if I had just stood there like the others, I would have . . . been no good to myself from then on" (quoted in Warren R. Young, "There's a Girl on the Tracks!" *Reader's Digest,* February 1977, pp.

91–95). You see, Everett Sanderson's dramatic actions were products of the promptings of his heart. That is what real courage is all about. He knew he must act accordingly or he would lose his self-worth. Real courage drives individuals to do what is right regardless of the circumstances, people involved, or consequences. Sir Winston Churchill once said, "The prime virtue in life is courage, because it makes all the other virtues possible." Considering the proper definition of *courage*—acting from the heart—I believe that Sir Winston Churchill was right.

Seasons

The Old Testament preacher, a son of David, taught that "to every thing there is a season, and a time to every purpose under the heaven" (Ecclesiastes 3:1). The Old Testament is filled with stories of individuals who were courageous when they *needed* to be courageous. During their season of courage, they seemed to recognize that it was now or never. Think of the courage required of Noah as he built the ark. This was not a weekend project but an enormous undertaking. Imagine the sarcastic remarks and public degradation as Noah labored not only to build a worthy boat but also to preach repentance to a rebellious people. Day by day Noah remained faithful as he continued this arduous task for some 120 years! (see Moses 8:16–17).

What about Abraham? Was he not a prime example of courage as he traveled to Mount Moriah with his only son, Isaac? Instructed to sacrifice his beloved son, Abraham marched steadily to the altar and even raised the knife necessary to perform the task. With the test complete, Isaac was spared and Abraham was declared a courageous man of God.

Think back to Joseph, son of Jacob who was later renamed Israel. His life was filled with many seasons that required courage. He was beaten, betrayed, and jailed. It seemed that every time things got a little better, disappointment raised its ugly head and bang, Joseph was in the dumps again. Yet with each new setback, Joseph grew a little taller, stronger, and braver. His circumstances were often changed, but his heart could not be conquered. His courage was deeply rooted.

Another example of devoted courage is Esther. Often considered a heroine of the Israelites, Esther was born in captivity, orphaned, and raised by her older cousin Mordecai. Eventually Esther became queen of Persia. Because of a plot to destroy the Jewish population, Esther intervened during a season that required the depth of her courage to save her people. Also, we cannot forget Daniel and his friends Shadrach, Meshach, and Abed-nego. Think of Isaiah, Hezekiah, and the many others who remained faithful to their hearts in seasons of conflict, fear, war, and destruction.

One of my favorite demonstrations of real courage is Joshua. After Moses left the children of Israel, it was Joshua who was to lead the children of Israel into the promised land. Many years prior to this event, it was Joshua who was a spy that entered into the land of Canaan and beheld the strength of the enemy. Only two of the spies brought favorable reports to Moses, one of which was the young Joshua. After forty years of wandering in the wilderness, all of the scouting party had died save two: Joshua and Caleb, the two faithful scouts who had courageously tried to rally the people so long ago. After all those years, it was now Joshua's responsibility to take the Israelites into the promised land. This was truly a season that required great courage on the part of the Israelites and especially from their newly appointed leader. How would you like to try and fill the shoes of Moses?

As Joshua prepares to enter Canaan, he is told: "Only be thou strong and very courageous, that thou mayest observe to do according to all the law" (Joshua 1:7). You see, the Lord's counsel and view of courage does not reflect *fashionable* courage. It requires one to follow what one knows is right, to observe to do according to the law. Again, the Lord reminds Joshua, "Be strong and of a good courage; be not afraid, neither be thou dismayed: for the Lord thy God is with thee whithersoever thou goest" (Joshua 1:9). The rest of the story is history.

So what is the forecast for our day? President Ezra Taft Benson has referred to our day as the day "when the temptations, responsibilities, and opportunities are the very greatest" ("A Message to the Rising Generation," *Ensign*, November 1977, p. 30). This statement reminds me of the opening lines of Charles Dickens's *A Tale of Two Cities*. "It was the best of times, it was the worst of times, it was the age of wisdom, it was the age of foolishness." Since this time period presents both wonderful opportunities and corrosive temptations all at once, it seems that now is the season that individuals must act in accordance with what they know to be right. Elder Dallin H. Oaks of the Quorum of the Twelve Apostles asked, "If members of our Church do not oppose immoral and pernicious practices, who will? If not now, when? We *can* make a difference! May God help us to do so" (Quoted in "Gambling is 'Morally Wrong, Politically Unwise,' says Elder Oaks," *Ensign*, March 1987, p. 77).

In 1905, Evan Stephens sat on a rock in City Creek Canyon in Salt Lake City pondering a sermon that he had just heard President Joseph F. Smith deliver at the tabernacle. President Smith talked about the importance of the rising generations of the Church. Brother Stephens was so moved by President Smith's sermon that he penned these words: "Shall the youth of Zion falter in defending truth and right? When the enemy assaileth, shall we shrink or shun the fight? No!" He penned verse after verse, along with a chorus: "True to the faith that our parents have cherished, true to the truth for which martyrs have perished, to God's command, soul, heart, and hand, faithful and true we will ever stand" ("True to the Faith," *Hymns*, no. 254). That song, written over ninety years ago, still calls us to stand in this season of great courage. If the youth of Zion do not stand for truth and right today, who will? If not now, when?

The Season for Courage

Since our current world, like the cowardly lion, confuses courage with sensation and heroes with acts of perceived greatness, we must remember what genuine courage is as we prepare to make our stand. By today's standards heroes range from subway rescuers to someone who excels in sports or can sing well. In reality, however, genuine courage and authentic heroes are something quite different. President Joseph F. Smith said: "Those things which we call extraordinary, remarkable, or unusual may make history, but they do not make real life. After all, to do well those things which God ordained to be the common lot of all mankind, is the truest greatness" ("Common-Place Things," *Juvenile Instructor*, 15 December 1905, p. 752).

Sometimes the need for courage arises when you least expect it. I remember hearing a principal from a local school talk about one of his students who was running for a student government office. The traditional process of election involved peer voting, academic achievement, and an interview with the principal, parents, peers, and school staff. One of the questions asked by the interview committee was: "What makes you different from the other candidates?" Without hesitation, this LDS young man spoke of his values learned in his family and church. He spoke about reverence, respect, taking responsibility for personal actions, being resourceful in solving problems, and never giving up. Perhaps for this young man, this wasn't a display of extraordinary valor or conspicuous bravery. Some may say this wasn't courage on display at all. To his principal, however, this was newsworthy. He told me how impressed he was with this young man's conviction and the courage it took to speak from the heart. As I listened to him talk about this student, I was impressed to see that values taught in families and Church meetings are not easily forgotten, at least by some. Perhaps this is what Christ meant when he taught: "For where your treasure is, there will your heart be also" (Matthew 6:21; 3 Nephi 13:21). What this young man treasured was in his heart. In a way, this young man was just like Joshua. He was strong and courageous so that he might observe to do according to his heart. Such a young man, in my estimation, is the real winner regardless of the outcome of the election, because he acted in the season of courage.

Sometimes our acts of courage have a profound impact on others. Not just by impressing others, like my principal friend, but in helping others find their courageous selves as well. Elder Vaughn J. Featherstone of the Seventy told of a friend who attended a party following a state championship basketball game. With her parents out of town, the young hostess brought some cigarettes into the room and passed around a pack. Elder Featherstone's friend watched as his friends took a cigarette and passed the pack down the line. As the cigarettes drew ever closer, his resolve began to falter. He reasoned: "Oh well, it's only one cigarette and I guess I can smoke with them." But when the pack was only one person away, this young man observed: "When the cigarettes went to the fellow right next to me, he said, 'No, thanks, I don't smoke,' and passed them on. The strength of the friend on my left gave me the courage to do what I really wanted to do all along. I said, 'No, thanks,' too." With gratitude he concluded: "The thing I have wondered through all these years is, what would have happened to me if I had been sitting on the other side of my friend?" (Quoted in *A Generation of Excellence*, [Salt Lake City: Bookcraft, 1975], pp. 169–70).

Your seemingly unseen courage in the proper season can literally preserve others. The Lord reminds us to "be not weary in well-doing, for ye are laying the foundation of a great work. And out of small things proceedeth that which is great" (D&C 64:33). My life has been significantly altered because of courageous individuals who have been *well-doing*.

There is little doubt that this is a season when we must make a stand. This is the season of courage. It is important to know that there are many courageous individuals of all ages living today. You are not alone. There are Davids, Josephs, Abrahams, and Esthers in our midst. I have met them. Many of you are fighting against almost unimaginable odds, but you're hanging in there. Some are fighting immorality, pornography, and other temptations that the world tries to pass off as no big deal. It is a big deal, and those who stand courageously will make a difference. I know youth who have families that are struggling, who are fighting terminal illnesses or trying to keep their head above water in the flood of apathy and sin. I marvel at their determination to make a stand. I admire their courage to be true to the faith.

In a season that is filled with the best of times and the worst of times, we must have courage, genuine courage to "be not afraid, neither be . . . dismayed" (Joshua 1:9). While speaking at a fireside to nearly ten thousand youth, President Gordon B. Hinckley read from letters written to him from seminary students. One letter, written by a young woman, shared her struggles to make right choices: "I do want you to know that I am a darned good kid. . . . I am so proud of my Church and my standards, which come from the Church. I am going the right direction. I don't know how much faith you have in the youth of the world today, but you can count on me. I will be on the front line when the time comes to fight the great battle, the final battle, because of my love for the Savior. I love you and all you stand for. I'll keep trying to do my best" (Quoted in "President Hinckley urges youth to choose right," *Church News*, 20 January 1994).

Shall the youth of Zion falter? Obviously not! Shall they shrink and shun the fight? I can assuredly declare no! The secret of standing in this season of courage is not in self-determination. Again we look to the Lord's advice to Joshua. With storm clouds gathering on the horizon and difficult times ahead, Joshua was told: "Be strong and of a good courage; be not afraid, neither be thou dismayed." Why? Here is the secret: "For the Lord thy God is with thee whithersoever thou goest" (Joshua 1:9). If you have the Lord with you, you will not, you cannot fail.

Matthew O. Richardson is an assistant professor at Brigham Young University in the Department of Church History and Doctrine. He served a mission to Denmark and holds a doctoral degree in educational leadership. Matt enjoys sports, travelling, and making Mickey Mouse pancakes on Saturday mornings. He is passionate about his family and the gospel. He and his wife, Lisa, have four children.

It Is Time to Stand

For some time now I have wanted to write a talk for young men. This talk would focus on the importance of honoring the priesthood. This chapter is that talk. So sisters, I am sorry, but this chapter is written to the young men of the Aaronic Priesthood. But wait. Just because it was written to the young men doesn't mean there isn't anything in it for you. Keep reading, and I think you will see what I mean.

As I said, I have wanted to write this chapter for some time. The idea first came to me a few years ago while I was participating in a youth conference in Tucson, Arizona. It was while I was at that conference that I came to better understand what it means for a young man to honor his priesthood. Let me explain.

When my friend, Jack Rose, and I arrived at the airport in Phoenix, Arizona, I could tell this was going to be a different youth conference. Waiting to pick us up was Sister Martha Ludwig. Even though I had never seen her before, she was easy to pick out from among the rest of the people waiting for arrivals. She had the glow. You know what I mean? You can tell when someone is living the gospel: they just glow. In Sister Ludwig's case this was no fifty-watt light bulb, it was a three-hundred watt halogen bulb, if you know what I mean. Sister Ludwig is an amazing lady with a real zeal for the gospel.

As we traveled to Tucson, Sister Ludwig enthusiastically outlined for us what was going to happen at the conference. As she did, I have to admit I was a bit nervous. She told us they wanted the

youth to have a King Benjamin-like experience. So the youth conference committee had decorated the gym to look like the outdoors. It
was complete with tents and a tower. As I said, it made me a bit nervous. The whole outdoor theme with me on a tower and all the
youth on the floor did not sound like the ideal teaching situation.
And to make it worse, I think the Scouts had built the tower to practice their knot tying! Scary, huh? In my mind, I could picture trying
to climb the tower. Then I could see it tumble to the ground while
all the youth exploded in laughter.

When we arrived at the church, things were just as Sister Ludwig
described, tower and all. She explained that they wanted the youth to
be in charge as much as possible. So when it was time for the conference to start, a young woman would offer the opening prayer. A musical number would follow. Then I would climb the tower to speak. I
have to admit I was even more nervous when Sister Ludwig finished
with her explanation. However, she seemed sure this would be awesome. So I took my place by the tower without any complaint.

As I sat there, I watched the youth come in, find places on the
floor, and begin to visit with each other. Seeing these wonderful
youth only increased my anxiety. When all the youth were assem-
bled, the young man conducting the meeting welcomed everyone
and announced the program. Following this, the young woman
assigned to pray rose and gave the opening prayer. A musical
number was supposed to follow the prayer, but nothing happened.
No one got up, and I began to get very uneasy. A minute or two went
by, and everyone started to get uneasy. I was about to climb the
tower to speak when one young man stood up in the middle of the
gym and, unannounced, sang a song titled, "I Will Stand for Truth
and Righteousness." As he sang everyone became still and the Spirit
flooded into the room. When he finished, you could have heard a
pin drop. I sat there thinking this was the most amazing thing I had
ever seen. But then a young woman stood up next to him, and
together they sang the song again. They sang the song a third time,
and this time they were joined by several youth on different instru-
ments. They continued to sing the song over and over. Each time
they did, they were joined by more and more youth. Eventually all of
the youth were standing and singing. I learned later that only a few

of the youth were assigned to participate in that musical number. However, because of the Spirit even those that had not been assigned to sing stood to join in the singing. It was one of the most amazing things I have ever witnessed. When they finished singing for the last time, everyone sat down reverently. It was incredible.

As I watched, I was reminded of one of my favorite stories from the Book of Mormon: the two thousand stripling warriors. As I thought about this story, I could see in my mind a group of concerned people gathered to discuss their state of affairs. It was a difficult time. The Lamanites had waged a vicious war against the Nephites, and at the time the Nephites were losing. Things looked bleak. Many cities had been lost. Witnessing all of this were the people of Ammon. These were the people who had been converted by the sons of Mosiah and had made a covenant not to ever fight again. As a result, the Nephites had to fight without their help. The people of Ammon did all they could to lend their support, but now things were critical. So they met to discuss their options.

The scriptures say, "When they saw the danger, and the many afflictions and tribulations which the Nephites bore for them, they were moved with compassion and were desirous to take up arms in the defence of their country. But behold, as they were about to take their weapons of war, they were overpowered by the persuasions of Helaman and his brethren, for they were about to break the oath which they had made. And Helaman feared lest by so doing they should lose their souls; therefore all those who had entered into this covenant were compelled to behold their brethren wade through their afflictions, in their dangerous circumstances at this time" (Alma 53:13–15).

Can you picture that scene in your mind? Can you see those people wanting to help but not knowing what to do? Imagine how difficult that must have been. The scriptures continue:

> But behold, it came to pass they had many sons, who had not entered into a covenant that they would not take their weapons of war to defend themselves against their enemies; therefore they did assemble themselves together at this time, as many as were able to take up arms, and they called themselves Nephites.

And they entered into a covenant to fight for the liberty of the Nephites, yea, to protect the land unto the laying down of their lives; yea, even they covenanted that they never would give up their liberty, but they would fight in all cases to protect the Nephites and themselves from bondage.

Now behold, there were two thousand of those young men, who entered into this covenant and took their weapons of war to defend their country.

And now behold, as they never had hitherto been a disadvantage to the Nephites, they became now at this period of time also a great support; for they took their weapons of war, and they would that Helaman should be their leader.

And they were all young men, and they were exceedingly valiant for courage, and also for strength and activity; but behold, this was not all—they were men who were true at all times in whatsoever thing they were entrusted.

Yea, they were men of truth and soberness, for they had been taught to keep the commandments of God and to walk uprightly before him. (Alma 53:16–21)

Can you visualize these young men?

Now, we don't know what else took place on that occasion. All we know is that these young men decided to fight. However, do you want to know what I think happened? I think it was a lot like that youth conference in Tucson. I think everyone was trying to decide what to do when one young man stood up. As he did, I imagine that the crowd became quiet. Then I imagine that young man saying something like, "I have never fought before, but I love my family and my freedom, and I didn't make that covenant, so I will fight." At this point, I see this young man's best friend standing up next to him. As he does he probably says, "I will fight too." Then another young man across the room stands up and says he will fight as well. Eventually one young man after another stands until two thousand young men are standing. Then I see the first young man looking at Helaman and saying, "We will fight if you will lead, for we will follow a prophet." Can you picture this? Can you see those young men standing, full of faith and willing to fight? It is awesome, isn't it?

My young friends who hold the Aaronic Priesthood, you have within you the same opportunity and capability as did these stripling warriors. We too are at war. This time, though, the war is spiritual rather that physical. Concerning this spiritual war, the Apostle Paul taught: "Finally, my brethren, be strong in the Lord, and in the power of his might. Put on the whole armour of God, *that ye may be able to stand* against the wiles of the devil. For we wrestle not against flesh and blood, but against principalities, against powers, against the rulers of the darkness of this world, against spiritual wickedness in high places. Wherefore take unto you the whole armour of God, that ye may be able to withstand in the evil day, and having done all, *to stand*" (Ephesians 6:10–13; emphasis added).

So, brethren, it is your time to stand. Just like that young man in the Tucson youth conference. It's time for you to stand just like those two thousand stripling warriors did so long ago. Just as they made a difference in their day and literally turned the tide of the war, you too can make a difference and turn the tide of the war we are in today. All you have to do is stand.

The prophet of our day, President Gordon B. Hinckley, gave the brethren of the Aaronic Priesthood a vision of what could happen if they would stand. After reading a proclamation he had received from a group of Aaronic Priesthood holders, he said: "What a different world this would be if every young man could and would sign such a statement of promise. There would be no lives wasted with drugs. There would be no gangs with children killing children and young men headed either for prison or death. Education would become a prize worth working for. Service in the Church would become an opportunity to be cherished. There would be greater peace and love in the homes of the people. There would be no viewing of pornography, no reading of sleazy literature. You would honor and respect the girls with whom you associate, and they would never have any fear of being alone with you in any set of circumstances. It would be as if the stripling warriors of Helaman had recruited the youth of the world to their way of living" ("To the Boys and to the Men," *Ensign*, November 1998, p. 52).

So, how can you respond to President Hinckley's challenge to stand? How can you stand the way those stripling warriors did? My answer is, strive to fulfill the purpose of the Aaronic Priesthood. This purpose is to:

1. Become converted to the gospel of Jesus Christ and live by its teachings.
2. Magnify priesthood callings and fulfill the responsibilities of his priesthood office.
3. Give meaningful service.
4. Prepare to receive the Melchizedek Priesthood and temple ordinances.
5. Commit to, prepare for, and serve an honorable full-time mission.
6. Prepare to become a worthy husband and father.

(*Church Handbook of Instructions, Book 2: Priesthood and Auxiliary Leaders* [1998], p. 177)

Let's take a closer look at each one of these aspects and see how they apply to everyday life.

First, what can you do to become converted to the gospel of Jesus Christ and live by its teachings? In Doctrine & Covenants 19:23 the Lord gives us a pattern to accomplish this: "Learn of me, and listen to my words; walk in the meekness of my Spirit, and you shall have peace in me." So, to become converted and live by the teachings of the gospel, we need to begin by learning of Christ. The best place to do that is through scripture study. Brethren, read your scriptures on your own. Read them with your family. Study them in your seminary, priesthood, and Sunday school classes. Learning of Christ will increase the influence of the Spirit in your life. Listen to the prompting you receive as a part of the influence of the Spirit. As you do, you will find yourself doing what the Savior would do; you will become converted and live by His teachings. In short, you will find yourself moving toward the first purpose of the Aaronic Priesthood. You will be standing.

Second, what does it mean for an Aaronic Priesthood holder to magnify priesthood callings and fulfill the responsibilities of his priesthood office? When you magnify something, you make it larger. What is it you want to make larger or to magnify? I think it is the Savior (see 3 Nephi 18:24). For example, as you administer the sacrament you can magnify the Savior for the members of your ward. How can you do this? Elder Jeffrey R. Holland of the Quorum of the Twelve Apostles said:

> In that sacred setting, we ask you young men of the Aaronic Priesthood to prepare and bless and pass these emblems of the Savior's sacrifice worthily and reverently. What a stunning privilege and sacred trust given at such a remarkably young age! I can think of no higher compliment heaven could pay you. We do love you. Live your best and look your best when you participate in the sacrament of the Lord's Supper.
>
> May I suggest that wherever possible a white shirt be worn by the deacons, teachers, and priests who handle the sacrament. For sacred ordinances in the Church we often use ceremonial clothing, and a white shirt could be seen as a gentle reminder of the white clothing you wore in the baptismal font and an anticipation of the white shirt you will soon wear into the temple and onto your missions.
>
> That simple suggestion is not intended to be pharisaic or formalistic. We do not want deacons or priests in uniforms or unduly concerned about anything but the purity of their lives. But how our young people dress can teach a holy principle to us all, and it certainly can convey sanctity. As President David O. McKay taught, a white shirt contributes to the sacredness of the holy sacrament (see Conference Report, Oct. 1956, p. 89). ("This Do in Remembrance of Me," *Ensign*, November 1995, p. 68)

Elder Dallin H. Oaks of the Quorum of the Twelve Apostles counseled those who administer the sacrament to not do anything that might distract from the Savior. Rather, Elder Oaks encouraged Aaronic Priesthood holders to magnify the Savior. Like Elder Holland, he admonished, "All who officiate in the sacrament—in preparing, administering, or passing—should be well groomed and modestly dressed, with nothing about their personal appearance that calls special attention to themselves. In appearance as well as actions, they should avoid distracting anyone present from full attention to the worship and covenant making that is the purpose of this sacred ordinance." Elder Oaks continued, "With the single exception of those priests occupied breaking the bread, all who hold the

Aaronic Priesthood should join in singing the sacrament hymn by which we worship and prepare to partake. No one needs that spiritual preparation more than the priesthood holders who will officiate in it. My young brethren, it is important that you sing the sacrament hymn. Please do so" ("The Aaronic Priesthood and the Sacrament," *Ensign*, November 1998, p. 40). By participating in the administration of the sacrament as Elder Holland and Elder Oaks have described, you can magnify the Savior. By doing this you magnify your calling. You stand.

Third, what does it mean to give meaningful service? I think Elder Joe J. Christensen of the Seventy answered this question best. He told members of the Aaronic Priesthood that the Savior was counting on them to be a champion to those in need. To illustrate, Elder Christensen shared the following examples:

> In a high school not far from here, a young mentally handicapped student we will call Frank wanted so much to be accepted by the popular crowd. He would follow them around, always on the outside looking in, hoping to be included but never achieving it.
>
> One day in the cafeteria, some of the more popular boys and girls encouraged Frank to get up on the table and dance. Thinking he would please them, he did it. In his awkward way, he twisted and twirled. The group yelled, clapped their hands, and laughed. They were laughing *at* him, and Frank thought they were laughing *with* him.
>
> A few tables away, Dave was eating lunch with a friend and watching it all. He courageously leaped up, faced that crowd of tormentors, and through clenched teeth said, "I've had as much of this as I can stand!" He helped Frank down and said, "Frank, you come and have lunch with us." . . .
>
> There are those who wake up every morning dreading to go to school, or even to a Church activity, because they worry about how they will be treated. You have the power to change their lives for the better. You are a bearer of the priesthood of God, and the Lord is counting on you to be a builder and give them a lift. Think less about yourself and more about the power you have to assist others, even those within your own family.
>
> A 14-year-old sister was all dressed up to go to a Young Women

activity at a time in her life when she felt very unsure about herself. She was quietly and self-consciously inching her way toward the front door, hoping not to be noticed by all the young men in the living room who were visiting with her older brother Russell. She was given a life-changing boost when her older brother interrupted his conversation and said to her in front of his friends, "My, Emily, you look pretty tonight!" A small thing? No. There are young women who claim that they would not have made it through those growing-up years without the encouragement and support of their older brothers. ("The Savior Is Counting on You," *Ensign*, November 1996, p. 39; emphasis in original)

Isn't that awesome? Being a champion to those in need is a powerful way to give meaningful service. When you give that kind of service, you truly stand tall.

Fourth, what does it mean to prepare to receive the Melchizedek Priesthood and temple ordinances? To see if you are standing tall in this area, consider the following questions:

What pictures do you have in your room? Do you have a picture of the temple? Have you sat down with your dad or another worthy priesthood bearer and discussed what it means to them to hold the Melchizedek Priesthood? Have you asked them what it means to them to receive the ordinances of the temple? Have you asked your mom what the priesthood and the temple mean to her? Remember, the stripling warriors were taught by their mothers.

Fifth, what does it mean to commit to, prepare for, and serve an honorable full-time mission? Read what Elder Christensen said about how important a mission is: "Modern prophets have taught that every young man who is physically and mentally able should prepare himself to serve an honorable mission. The Lord did not say, 'Go on a mission if it fits your schedule, or if you happen to feel like it, or if it doesn't interfere with your scholarship, your romance, or your educational plans.' Preaching the gospel is a commandment and not merely a suggestion. It is a blessing and a privilege and not a sacrifice. Remember, even though for some of you there may be very tempting reasons for you not to serve a full-time mission, the Lord and his prophets are counting on you" ("The Savior is Counting on You," p. 41).

Brethren, if you haven't already committed to serve a mission, do it now. Do not wait another minute; commit now. Write that commitment down. Put it where you will see it often. The commitment to serve a mission is a commitment to stand. Your preparation will determine just how committed you are. Speaking of how you can best prepare, Elder L. Tom Perry of the Quorum of the Twelve Apostles said, "Your preparation must have you ready to sit in front of your bishop and certify to him of your personal worthiness to be a full-time missionary" ("Called to Serve," *Ensign*, May 1991, p. 39). Show the Lord you are committed to serve a mission by doing all you can to prepare now.

Finally, what does it mean to prepare to become a worthy husband and father? It seems to me that the best way to do this would be to keep your life clean. Concerning this, President Hinckley said: "A week ago President Faust and the Young Women general presidency spoke to the young women of the Church in this tabernacle. As I looked at that gathering of beautiful young women the question moved through my mind, 'Are we rearing a generation of young men worthy of them?'. . . The girl you marry will take a terrible chance on you. She will give her all to the young man she marries. . . . [Y]ou have a tremendous obligation toward the girl you marry. . . . The girl you marry can expect you to come to the marriage altar absolutely clean. She can expect you to be a young man of virtue in thought and word and deed. . . . The girl you marry is worthy of a husband whose life has not been tainted by . . . ugly and corrosive material. . . . Young men, now is the time to prepare for the future. And in that future for most of you is a beautiful young woman whose greatest desire is to bond with you in a relationship that is eternal and everlasting" ("Living Worthy of the Girl You Will Someday Marry," *Ensign*, May 1998, pp. 49, 51). Brethren, keep yourselves clean. If you have made mistakes, do what is necessary to repent. Then move forward with renewed commitment.

In a way, the purpose of the Aaronic Priesthood represents a measuring stick to help you see how tall you are standing. Measuring up can seem a bit overwhelming. In fact, there will be times when you feel like you are far short of where you should be. When you feel this way, remember those stripling warriors. They stood tall.

They were able to measure up. However, there was not one of them that did not receive many wounds in the attempt. So how did they do it? With the Savior's help. He will help you stand tall.

Remember that Heavenly Father would not require so much of you if He didn't think you were capable of accomplishing the purpose of the Aaronic Priesthood. As you do your best and trust in your Savior, you will stand like that young man at the youth conference in Tucson. You will stand like the stripling warriors. As you do, eventually you will help yourselves, your families, your friends, and your communities defeat the powers of darkness that are so abundant today. Helaman asked the stripling warriors, "Therefore what say ye, my sons, will ye go against them to battle?" (Alma 56:44). Will you stand?

R. Scott Simmons was born and raised in Salt Lake City, Utah. He spent his summers working on a dairy farm and is a real cowboy at heart. He served a mission in Cleveland, Ohio. Following his mission he attended BYU and worked at the Missionary Training Center. He currently teaches seminary at Timpview High School in Provo, Utah. Scott loves the outdoors and spends as much time as possible  *hunting, fishing, and camping. Scott and his wife, Nancy, live in Highland, Utah.*

The Young Women Theme:
A Source of Courage and Strength

Since this chapter is about the Young Women theme, it may not seem applicable to the young men. However, even though I'll be addressing mainly the ladies, the men may also want to read for the following reasons: (1) This isn't frilly stuff. The values in the theme are based on sound doctrine and scriptures that were written for all of us. Every Young Women value can be found in part or in its entirety in the Topical Guide, along with numerous scriptural references. (2) Your mothers, future wives, sisters, female friends, and cousins have probably been through the Young Women program. Wouldn't it be great to know a little about what they spent those six years learning? (3) Last but not least, I know a lot of men who have the Young Women theme memorized. That's impressive, especially since they might be fathers of daughters someday if not already. I've included the theme in its entirety at the end of this chapter.

Now ladies, since we're already familiar with the theme, our focus is a little bit different from the men's. As you are reading, try to think about—I mean really think about—what it means to be a daughter of God and what you're actually saying when you stand and repeat the theme each Sunday. I recently was released after serving for two years as a Young Women leader in my ward. Each week we would recite the Young Women theme together. Each week, as I watched preoccupied faces and fidgety fingers, I wondered if these young women knew what they were really saying and how it could be a great source of strength in their lives.

So much power is packed in the very first sentence of the theme alone: "We are daughters of our Heavenly Father, who loves us, and we love Him" (*Church Handbook of Instructions, Book 2: Priesthood and Auxiliary Leaders* [1998], p. 211). Our Heavenly Father loves us completely and individually as his daughters. He loves us enough to have sent his Only Begotten Son to suffer and die so that we might live with them again. Next time you begin the theme, think about how much you personally are loved by Him. Elder Melvin J. Ballard of the Quorum of the Twelve Apostles helped us understand the depth of our Father's feeling for us when He gave us His son, our Savior: "In that hour I think I can see our dear Father behind the veil looking upon these dying struggles until even he could not endure it any longer; and, like the mother who bids farewell to her dying child, has to be taken out of the room, so as not to look upon the last struggles, so he bowed his head, and hid in some part of his universe, his great heart almost breaking for the love that he had for his Son. Oh, in that moment when he might have saved his Son, I thank him and praise him that he did not fail us, for he had not only the love of his Son in mind, but he also had love for us. I rejoice that he did not interfere, and that his love for us made it possible for him to endure to look upon the sufferings of his Son and give him finally to us, our Savior and our Redeemer. Without him, without his sacrifice, we would have remained, and we would have never come glorified into his presence. And so this is what it cost, in part, for our Father in Heaven to give the gift of his Son unto men" (Quoted in Bryant S. Hinckley, *Sermons and Missionary Services of Melvin Joseph Ballard* [Salt Lake City: Deseret Book Co., 1949], pp. 154–55).

I can only imagine our Father's anguish as the Savior suffered during the process of the Atonement. The love that we speak of in the Young Women theme between a Father and a daughter motivates us to make the commitment, "We will 'stand as witnesses of God at all times and in all things, and in all places' (Mosiah 18:9) as we strive to live the Young Women values" (*Church Handbook*, p. 211) Did you notice that little word *all*? It has only three letters, but together they pack a strong punch. Did you also notice that the word is included three times? I believe the women who wrote the theme were truly inspired, and it leaves no confusion about what is expected of us. At this point, it's probably important to also mention the word *strive*. The theme does not say we should be perfect in living the Young Women values. It says, "As we *strive* to live the Young Women values." Each of us has and will make mistakes, as Jesus Christ was the only perfect person to come to earth, but I do think *strive* means more than just "try." When someone says "I'll try," it sometimes leaves you with that I-doubt-it-will-ever-happen feeling. Strive, on the other hand, means work, sweat, and sometimes tears as we continually repent and make the changes necessary to come closer to our Savior. It's interesting that each of the Young Women values contained within the theme helps us to do just that. In an uncertain, challenging world, living the Young Women values provides courage to keep the commandments, which are a veritable lifeline to Christ.

Faith is the first value in the list. When asked what faith is, we can all generally spout the answer that "Faith is to hope for things which are not seen," as stated in scriptures and in the Bible Dictionary. We've heard it many times, but did you know that the Bible Dictionary has sixty more lines after this first one that continue to define faith? We generally think of faith as a thought or feeling, yet the Bible Dictionary tells us that it is a principle of power and of action: "Miracles do not produce faith but strong faith is developed by obedience to the gospel of Jesus Christ" ("Faith," p. 669).

I've heard some young people say that they don't keep the principles of the gospel because they just don't know it is true. How unfortunate. They may never know, because testimony is based on faith in the Savior, and faith is gained by being obedient to the Savior's commandments. In the Book of Mormon, Alma tells us that our faith needs to be nourished from a tiny seed to become a great tree (see Alma 32). Obedient actions coupled with prayer will do the nourishing, but waiting for a testimony to instantaneously appear won't. If we cultivate our faith, even if it is built slowly it will be a ray of light that can pull us through some of the darkest times. President Brigham Young said, "The faith I have embraced has given me light for darkness, ease for pain, joy and gladness for sorrow and mourning, certainty for uncertainty, hope for despair" (in *Journal of Discourses,* 9:318).

Next in the list of values are *Divine Nature* and *Individual Worth.* Isn't it wonderful that we have the light of Christ? Years ago, while I was studying in Israel, I entered a shop in Jerusalem with some friends. The shopkeeper approached us and said, "You are Mormons." I asked how he knew this, and he replied, "I can tell by the light in your faces." Our nature truly is divine. We have the light of Christ and heavenly parents as well as earthly parents. I have heard many Christians say that we are all children of God. This statement is monumental. Our divine nature makes us of infinite, individual worth. But if we know this is true, then why do so many young women struggle with esteem and self-worth? I think we often judge ourselves by the world's standards. With the onslaught of mass-media messages, we lose sight of the fact that we are daughters of a Heavenly Father who loves us and members of a church that is worth working for. Instead, we're barraged with messages telling us how we should look, dress, and feel, what our household roles, occupations, and even choices of beverage say about our identity. We're in a no-waiting, fast-food, minimal-assembly-required world. Good grief! No wonder people are confused and have unrealistic expectations that often lead to disappointment.

Patricia T. Holland, a former member of the Young Women general presidency, commented on this very issue:

> We *must* have the courage to be imperfect while striving for perfection. We *must* not allow our own guilt, the feminist books, the talk-show hosts, or the whole media culture to sell us a bill of goods—or rather a bill of *no* goods. We can become so sidetracked in our compulsive search for identity and self-esteem that we really believe it *can* be found in having perfect figures or academic degrees or professional status or even absolute motherly success. Yet, in so searching externally, we can be torn from our true internal, eternal selves. We often worry so much about pleasing and performing for others that we lose our uniqueness—that full and relaxed acceptance of one's self as a person of worth and individuality. . . . Often we fail to consider the glorious possibility within our own souls. We need to remember that

divine promise, 'The Kingdom of God is within you.' (Luke 17:21.) Perhaps we forget that the kingdom of God is within us because too much attention is given to this outer shell, this human body of ours, and the frail, too-flimsy world in which it moves. ("'One Thing Needful': Becoming Women of Greater Faith in Christ," *Ensign*, October 1987, pp. 29–30, 31; emphasis in original)

Knowledge is fourth. Knowledge is power. Spiritual knowledge, particularly, gives us the power of discernment and the ability to make wise choices. I know without question or wavering that spiritual knowledge is the most important knowledge that we can gain on this earth. Our Heavenly Father wants us to learn of our Savior and study and ponder the scriptures daily. In the Old Testament, we read that Eve, the mother of all living, was commanded to multiply and replenish the earth. The word *multiply* is pretty straightforward, but what does it mean to replenish? It means to make more complete and, I think, better. As young women in the gospel and future mothers, we need to be prepared to raise up a righteous generation. This is our most important and sacred responsibility as women. We must replenish, or make better, the world by living righteous lives and teaching our children to do the same.

In the scriptures, another word for Jesus Christ is light. How can we fill the world with light if we don't know the light ourselves? It takes more than just reading the word of the Lord to come to know him, it also involves serious thought, consideration, and prayer. I found an example of this on a sleepless Christmas night. After tossing and turning for quite some time, I rolled out of bed, plugged in the Christmas-tree lights, and pulled out my scriptures. While rereading Luke's account of the Savior's birth, I stopped on verses 18 and 19 of chapter two: "And all they that heard it [the account of the angels' visit and the birth of the Christ child] wondered at those things which were told them by the shepherds. But Mary kept all these things, and pondered them in her heart." If you look at the footnote for the word *wondered*, it suggests the alternative word *marvelled*, and if you look at the footnote for the word *pondered*, it refers the reader to "Meditation" in the Topical Guide, where related topics include "Think," "Prayer," and "Scriptures, Study of" (p. 314). After hearing the angel tell her that she would bear the Savior of mankind, I'm sure Mary felt the weight of the world as she held her infant son. However, I'm sure she also felt a joy beyond anything we can imagine because she knew her son would also be her Redeemer. The mother of the Savior pondered the things of Christ in her heart and gave us an example to follow as we prepare to become mothers ourselves. If we are to teach our children of Christ, we must study, ponder, and pray so that we first may have a knowledge of Him.

Spiritual knowledge must be our priority, but we should also remember the importance of education and formal learning. As a teacher, I try to show my students that skills in reading, writing, math, science, art, technology, and other important subjects will help them survive and succeed in an ever-changing, advancing world. Gaining a marketable skill will allow them to provide for themselves and their future families if necessary. For example, my own father was struck by lightning and killed when I was two years old. My mother had to go back to college and finish her degree so she could provide for our family. She used her formal knowledge and skills to meet our material needs, but she used her faith and knowledge of the Savior to meet our spiritual needs. When you say the word *knowledge* in the theme, think about President Brigham Young's wise counsel: "After all our endeavors to obtain wisdom from the best books, etc., there still remains an open fountain for all; 'If any man lack wisdom let him ask of God.' . . . [I]f you live so as to possess the Holy Ghost . . . you will at once see the difference between the wisdom of men and the wisdom of God, and you can weigh things in the balance and estimate them at their true worth" (John A. Widtsoe, ed., *Discourses of Brigham Young,* [Salt Lake City: Bookcraft, 1998], pp. 261, 323).

Choice and Accountability follows *knowledge* in the Young Women theme. As women, we are living in a world where more options are available to us than at any other time in history. This is exciting but also increases the importance of making wise personal choices. One of the basic principles in the plan of salvation is agency. We, along with two-thirds of the hosts of heaven, agreed to come to earth and be accountable to ourselves and our Father in Heaven. If you look under "Agency" in the Topical Guide, it says, *"See also . . . Accountability"*

(p. 8). It stands to reason that accountability should also be part of the Young Women value regarding choice. There is a consequence, whether good or bad, to every decision we make. I once attended a United Nations World Youth Summit in Portugal, which was also attended by youth representatives from all over the world. The rights of youth were vehemently discussed, yet there was little talk of the responsibility that always accompanies freedom, rights, and choice. Choice and accountability are inextricably connected. Put simply, we must, as witnesses of God, think before we speak or act. I cannot imagine Lucifer's concept of a world without choice. At the same time, I think it's ironic that this very principle of the gospel is so often twisted to promote his purposes. Think about the abortion campaign slogan of "pro-choice." I wonder if people might think of that slogan differently if the words *and pro-accountability* were added to the billboards next to the word pro-choice. We live in a wonderful time of opportunity and choice, but it is up to us to remember that we are also accountable for the choices we make.

The next value is *Good Works*. In President Gordon B. Hinckley's 1998 Christmas message, I remember him mentioning that we should be just as anxious about the good things we *should* be doing as we are about the not-so-good things we may have done. Wouldn't it be great if each Sunday when we said the Good Works part of the theme, we decided upon specific good works to do that week and then actually did them? I have mentioned already that I am a teacher. I get excited when I see young people at our junior high school doing kind things for each other. However, I literally get a knot in the pit of my stomach when I see the suffering some students endure. A few years ago, I had a student who used to stay in my classroom for hours after school because she didn't want to go home. I used to wish she could make some friends. When I assigned the seating chart, the other kids at her table would run up and ask to be moved because they didn't like the way she smelled. I would try to pick the kindest kids in the class to sit by her in hopes that they might include her, but sometimes even they complained. When it was time to pick teams or do group work, she was the last to be chosen. I used to think, *What are you people doing? She is the one who should be chosen first; who needs to be chosen first.* I wish that

I could say this was an isolated incident, but I've seen many similar situations.

Fortunately, I also see stellar young people who go out of their way to be kind to others and do good works. We need more of them. When we say the Good Works part of the theme, we could even go a step further and recommit ourselves to making good works become a part of our general nature rather than isolated incidents or service projects. I'm embarrassed to admit that when I was young, I stood by while some kids were mistreating a girl in our neighborhood. I didn't join in, but I didn't stand up for her or go out of my way to befriend her, either. Her older sister pulled me aside and asked why I was not helping her sister. I shrugged. She said, "That's not like you, Cindy. That's just not like you." That statement rang true to every fiber of my being. I knew she was right and decided that being a part of the crowd was not worth being untrue to myself and the actions I knew to be good. Elder Neal A. Maxwell of the Quorum of the Twelve Apostles said: "Crowds cannot make right what God has declared to be wrong" ("'Answer Me,'" *Ensign*, November 1988, p. 33). I wish I could say that I've always treated people with good works rather than bad works or even no works at all. I haven't, but I do strive to make it a priority.

Finally, *Integrity* ends the list of Young Women values. Are our actions always in line with our beliefs and values? Sometimes when we lack integrity, it's because we lack faith. We worry more about consequences and what others think than about doing what is right and honest. Esther in the Old Testament is a stunning example of integrity. As queen, she had been asked to approach the king on behalf of her people because there had been a decree that all Jews should be put to death. She says, "All the king's servants . . . know, that whosoever, whether man or woman, shall come unto the king into the inner court, who is not called, there is one law of his to put him to death, except such to whom the king shall hold out the golden sceptre, that he may live: but I have not been called to come in unto the king these thirty days" (Esther 4:11). Esther had reason to be afraid. Not only was she afraid of displeasing the king, but she knew her own life was at stake. However, she used her faith to combat her fear and gain courage. She says in verse 16, "Go, gather together all the Jews that are present in Shushan, and fast ye for me, and neither eat nor drink three days, night or day: I also and my maidens will fast likewise; and so will I go in unto the king, which is not according to the law: and if I perish, I perish." What a courageous woman. She did go to the king, and her life and the lives of her people were spared. It is not always easy to have integrity, but faith makes it possible to have courage when faced with hard decisions. In the future, we can call upon Esther's example of integrity when we're in tough situations. We can choose the right even if we then must say, "If I fail, I fail. If I'm unpopular, I'm unpopular. If I perish, I perish." This truly is a season for courage. Be strong and courageous in doing what you know is right. Decide each Sunday when you repeat the theme to commit to be a person of integrity, a person of courage.

We end the theme by saying, "We believe as we come to accept and act upon these values, we will be prepared to make and keep sacred covenants, receive the ordinances of the temple, and enjoy the blessings of exaltation" (*Church Handbook,* p. 211). If we are true to the Young Women theme and live by it rather than just say it, we will enjoy the blessings of exaltation. Elder James E. Talmage of the Quorum of the Twelve Apostles wrote specifically for young women about these eternal blessings in the *Young Women's Journal* in 1914: "When the frailties and imperfections of mortality are left behind, in the glorified state of the blessed hereafter, husband and wife will administer in their respective stations, seeing and understanding alike, and co-operating to the full in the government of their family kingdom. Then shall woman be recompensed in rich measure for all the injustice that womanhood has endured in mortality. Then shall woman reign by Divine right, a queen in the resplendent realm of her glorified state, even as exalted man shall stand, priest and king unto the Most High God. Mortal eye cannot see nor mind comprehend the beauty, glory, and majesty of a righteous woman made perfect in the celestial kingdom of God" (Quoted in Andrew F. Ehat and Lyndon W. Cook, ed., *The Words of Joseph Smith* [Salt Lake City: Bookcraft, 1980], p. 137, note 4).

That passage was written a long time ago yet still paints a beautiful picture today of what we can look forward to if we are righteous while on this earth. Living the Young Women theme will help us to achieve these blessings, as will the mercy of the Savior's Atonement. The theme is inspired, timely, and will give us courage and strength in an uncertain season. I'm grateful we can stand each week and proclaim:

> We are daughters of our Heavenly Father, who loves us, and we love Him. We will "stand as witnesses of God at all times and in all things, and in all places" (Mosiah 18:9) as we strive to live the Young Women values, which are: Faith, Divine Nature, Individual Worth, Knowledge, Choice and Accountability, Good Works, and Integrity. We believe as we come to accept and act upon these values, we will be prepared to make and keep sacred covenants, receive the ordinances of the temple, and enjoy the blessings of exaltation. (*Church Handbook*, p. 211)

Cindy Bishop Grace was born in Rochester, New York, and raised in Sandy, Utah. She served a service mission in Nauvoo, Illinois. She graduated from Brigham Young University with a BA in communications education, and is currently an English teacher at Oak Canyon Jr. High and an adjunct faculty member at BYU. She loves traveling with her husband, Jeff, and singing and reading to her supersocial two-year-old, Katie.

Pornography: Satan's Counterfeit

In 1996 the United States Treasury issued a new design of the hundred-dollar bill. I never saw it because Ben Franklin and I don't spend a lot of time together, but when the new fifties and twenties started showing up a few years later I got to examine some new currency. "It looks like play money," I told the bank teller. "I feel like we're starting a Monopoly game."

"It's real," she assured me.

"Why did they change it?" I asked.

She explained that in our high-tech society it was becoming much too easy to counterfeit the former bills. "These new notes have more security features built in." she said. "It's easier to spot the forgeries."

It's good they made the change. I wouldn't want to get stuck with any counterfeit bills. I once read of a man who spent several days helping to unload, clean, and reload a huge truck, only to be paid in counterfeit money. At first he didn't notice. In fact, he was excited because he thought the truck driver had been extremely generous. The man thanked the driver profusely as he left. Then the man tried to buy something at a store. The cashier took his money, looked at it, and called over the manager. The manager examined the bills and told the man his money was unacceptable.

Suddenly the guy wasn't feeling so grateful to that truck driver. In fact, he was furious. He couldn't believe the driver would intentionally deceive him. He was embarrassed in front of the cashier and store manager. He felt bitter, angry, and discouraged that he had nothing to show for his time and effort but a handful of worthless forgeries.

When I read that story, I felt sorry for the man but not nearly as sorry as I feel for young people who get stuck with a different kind of forgery. The man lost some money. Some young people I know are in danger of losing a lot more because they are accepting a counterfeit from Satan called pornography.

What is more beautiful than the human body? What is more wonderful and pure than true love between husband and wife? These sacred things have incredible eternal value. No wonder Satan tries to counterfeit them. Are we going to accept his cheap imitations? Are we going to let Satan rip us off?

Not many of us can spot a counterfeit bill. At first many do not recognize Satan's frauds either. Like the man who was excited to receive the truck driver's money, too many get excited about pornography only to find out later that what they assumed to be worthwhile is actually worthless.

One LDS young man I'll call Matt became involved with pornography when he was visiting at a friend's house and his friend showed him some magazine pictures. Matt says, "I had always heard pornography described as dirty, smutty, filthy, and ugly. But what I saw in those pictures didn't look all that ugly to me. It looked pretty appealing." Matt allowed himself to be fooled. He found himself tempted to view pornography more and more. He started to buy magazines, rent videos, and look up pornographic sites on the Internet. Matt says, "It wasn't hard to find once I started looking."

In the months that followed, Matt found himself less and less satisfied with the soft stuff. He says, "I wanted pictures that were more graphic and extreme." He soon found that his unworthy thoughts led to unworthy acts, one after another after another. Matt says, "I let my hormones override all my better judgment. Guilt, fear, and depression became my constant companions: guilt because I knew what I was doing was wrong; fear because I was terrified that my secret indulgences would be found out; and depression because I could no longer feel the Spirit. I began to hate myself."

Matt was caught in a dangerous downward cycle. In an effort to ease his depression, he would view pornography. Then he would become more depressed than before and once again turn to the pornography as a temporary escape. Matt explains, "I first started viewing pornography because it was exciting and gave me a rush. Later I no longer turned to pornography to feel good, but to stop from feeling bad." He was hooked. Just as surely as if he were heavily involved with drugs or alcohol, he was addicted.

Matt says, "Over and over I'd tell myself that I would never view pornography again. Then I'd go right ahead and do it." Like the man who received counterfeit bills from the truck driver, Matt realized that what he originally thought was something good was just a fake. Like the man, Matt felt embarrassed, bitter, and angry. He says, "I think of the time and money I spent on that stuff, and I feel sick. It affected my relationships with others, my Church activity, and my grades in school. It consumed my life, and I feel angry about that, but I know I have no one to blame but myself."

Empty-handed, broken-hearted, Matt finally found the courage to approach his bishop. With the help of his priesthood leader, he began the long process of repenting and breaking unworthy habits. Matt states, "Turning away from pornography has been the most difficult thing I have ever done. Sometimes it is such a battle to control my thoughts that by the end of the day I feel physically, emotionally, and spiritually drained. I would give anything if I had never started in the first place." I admire Matt's determination to repent and make positive changes. I appreciate him letting me share his story. He says, "Perhaps it can help others be smarter than I was. Maybe it can help them avoid my struggles."

How do we avoid getting sucked in? If some, like Matt, have been tempted in the past, how can unworthy habits be broken once and for all? The new money issued by the United States Treasury has security features. That's what we need too: ways to detect and reject Satan's counterfeit of pornography. On each new bill there is an enlarged portrait, a new background, glowing thread, microprinting, a number that shifts color when viewed from different angles, and a watermark that is visible when held to the light.

Enlarged Portrait

The enlarged portrait on the bills allows for more detail, which makes it harder to duplicate them. As we seek for power to reject pornography, it helps to have an enlarged picture of ourselves, the details about who we are eternally and our role in Heavenly Father's plan.

Consider the significance of receiving, caring for, and honoring our bodies, bodies for which we longed during our premortal experience, bodies that Satan and his hosts will never have. No wonder they want us to disregard, disrespect, and abuse our own bodies and the bodies of others.

Consider the sacred nature of our procreative powers. Think of how the righteous use of these powers can bring us to God as he allows us to have families of our own. Within marriage, sexual relations are a wholesome tool that can be used to build incredible loving relationships between husbands and wives who are bonded together spiritually and emotionally as well as physically. No wonder Satan will do anything to degrade sex and tempt us to use that tool to destroy instead of build. Satan would have us use the very power that can bring us such unbelievable joy in unauthorized and selfish ways. He would have us settle for fleeting gratification over enduring happiness. We must keep an enlarged portrait of our eternal potential firmly in our minds. Then Satan's counterfeit can be seen for what it is.

New Background

Each new bill also has a new background behind the enlarged portrait. When trying to resist any temptation, it is helpful to modify our background, or environment. If I am trying to lose weight, I'd better not be hanging around the bakery. Similarly, those trying to quit drinking are foolish to enter bars. Those struggling with pornography must not allow themselves to go near certain stores or into the homes of certain friends. They would be wise to move their computers out of their bedrooms and into more public places, such as the living room or family room. If laptops present too great a temptation, it may be wise to get a parental protection program or an Internet filter and let someone else control the password.

The new backgrounds on the money are filled with lines. We must fill our new environments with lots of people and positive activities. When all else fails, in moments of temptation we need to follow the example of Joseph of old and simply run away (see Genesis 39:12). Then we will be more secure against Satan's counterfeit.

Microprinting

If you look closely at the new bills, you will see tiny words printed throughout the side borders and portraits. On the fifty-dollar bill, for example, take a good look at Grant's collar. Because the words are so small, microprinting is hard to duplicate and thus offers greater security. Isn't that the same in our lives? It's the little things that make the difference.

When my daughter was in second grade, we were having family night and I asked, "What can we do to be happy?" After a long pause she exhaled loudly, rolled her eyes dramatically, and sighed, "Just . . . just do . . . all that stuff!"

At first I thought she was being silly, but the more I thought about it, the more I realized she was absolutely right. By "all that stuff" she meant to pray and read scriptures, Church-oriented books, and the *New Era* (and not just the joke page). We need to fast, bear our testimony, attend Church meetings, participate in Young Men and Young Women activities, and stay close to our parents and leaders. Sure, they are all small things, but "by small and simple things are great things brought to pass" (Alma 37:6).

Glowing Thread

The polymer thread that has been embedded vertically in the paper of the new bills glows yellow under ultraviolet light. This makes any counterfeit extremely easy to spot because it doesn't have a glowing thread. Similarly, a marriage that has been embedded with threads of trust, fidelity, and commitment glows with love. There is no love in pornography, only lust. There is no concern for another, only for self. There is no relationship to be strengthened, only nameless bodies, dehumanized sexual objects. Victor B. Cline stated that most pornography "presents highly inaccurate, unscientific, and distorted information about human sexuality. It is, in a sense, sex miseducation marketed for financial gain" (in Daniel H. Ludlow, ed., *Encyclopedia of Mormonism,* 5 vols. [New York: Macmillan Publishing Co., 1992], 3:1112). Where there is no love, there is no glow, and Satan's bill is seen for the dull, dark, and lifeless counterfeit it is.

Color Shifting

The numbers in the lower right corners of the new bills are printed in such a way that they appear green when viewed from straight on but black when viewed from an angle. It's called color shifting. Many in the world would try to convince us there are no absolutes when it comes to good or bad, that right and wrong exist only in our minds and that what is moral or immoral depends completely on the angle from which it is viewed. Don't be fooled. The shifting colors on the new bills provide security, but the shifting values of the world do not. From any angle pornography is wrong and sinful.

President Spencer W. Kimball stated, "Pornography pollutes the mind. The stench of obscenity and vulgarity reaches and offends the heavens. It putrifies all it touches . . . . Pornography and erotic stories and pictures are worse than polluted food. Shun them. The body has power to rid itself of sickening food. That person who entertains filthy stories or pornographic pictures and literature records them in his marvelous human computer, the brain, which can't forget this filth" (Edward L. Kimball, ed., *The Teachings of Spencer W. Kimball* [Salt Lake City: Bookcraft, 1982], pp. 282–83).

I once attended a youth conference and stayed as a guest in the home of one of the adult leaders. This good brother and his wife made arrangements for their teenage son to stay over with friends so I could sleep in his room. As they led me upstairs, they apologized because their son, a priest, had chosen to cover the walls of his room with pictures of models and actresses wearing not much more than smiles. The father said, "I've talked to him, but he says I'm making a big deal out of nothing, that all his school friends do the same thing and the pictures are really not that bad."

The words brought to my mind some questions Elder Richard G. Scott of the Quorum of the Twelve Apostles asked during a talk at BYU: "Do you thirst after righteousness? Or are there times when the allure of stimulating images is allowed to temporarily fill your mind because, after all, they are really not that bad? Do your actions focus on entertainment, immediate satisfaction, self-interests, or personal gratification even though your goals are elsewhere?" ("Finding Happiness," in *1996–7 Speeches* [Provo, Utah: Brigham Young University Publications and Graphics, 1997], p. 360).

I left my bags in the room and went to the youth conference. Later that night when I returned to my host family's home and entered the young man's bedroom, I was immediately confronted by all the supposedly not-so-bad images and decided to take matters into my own hands. I found some paper and scissors and cut out a lot of circles like the ones you see coming from the mouths of cartoon characters in the comics. I then taped the paper bubbles next to the mouths of all the ladies and wrote comments like, "I'm going to marry only a returned missionary," "I want to be married in the temple," and "I am a daughter of my Father in Heaven, who loves me, and I love him."

The next day when the boy saw the pictures, he got quite a kick out of my creativity. I apologized for redecorating his room, and we parted friends. I didn't realize the impact my practical joke would have until later when the boy wrote me the following: "At first I took what you did in my room as a big joke. I even invited a bunch of kids from youth conference to come see your masterpieces. Everyone thought they were pretty funny. But then I started to really think about what you had written on those papers. It's true. Those girls are daughters of Heavenly Father, and I certainly haven't been looking at them that way. To see words about temple marriage on those kind of posters seemed so inconsistent. Suddenly it hit me that by having those pictures up on my walls I was being inconsistent too. Needless to say, the posters came down."

Many attempt to rationalize poor choices by saying things like,

"Everybody does it," "It's not that big a deal," "I can handle it," "It doesn't really affect me," "It's nothing I haven't seen before." Some even try to claim that the pornography they view is art. I remember taking an art history class at BYU in which we occasionally studied paintings or statues of nudes. When the instructor was asked if such pieces were pornographic, he explained the difference by defining two words: sensuous and sensual. He said nudity in art can be sensuous because its beauty appeals to the senses, while pornography is sensual because its only purpose is erotic arousal for commercial gain. The instructor's distinction has helped me a great deal in my own life as I draw the important lines between art and pornography, literature and lewdness.

When it comes to pornography, we must never open the door even the slightest crack, for as the ancient sage Rabbi Isaac once said of evil: "At first it is a wayfarer and a lodger. At last it becomes the master of the house" (Jon R. Haddon, "An Urge Toward Evil," *Reader's Digest,* November 1998, p. 48).

Watermark Visible in the Light

The new bill has a watermark that is clearly visible from both sides when held to the light. The security of those who struggle with pornography will likewise be more sure when they are willing to hold their actions to the light by seeking help. Those who have courage to admit their struggle to a bishop find a valuable friend and ally. In private interviews some bishops will ask directly about pornography; others won't. Either way, it's up to those who struggle to bring their problem to light.

A commitment made to yourself can easily be broken. Commitments to God are often too easily postponed. But when commitments are made to another person, it puts on some pressure. It's pretty obvious that a person who arranges to exercise with a friend usually hangs in there longer than someone who does not. When the alarm goes off in the morning, it's easy to turn it off and roll over unless you know someone is waiting for you. Research studies have shown that those who make public commitments to quit smoking have a much greater chance of succeeding than those who try to do it secretly. Patients who make written commitments to take pre-scribed medicine are much more likely to follow through than patients who do not. When those who struggle with pornography know they will be seeing a bishop on Sunday morning, it may help them think twice about what they do on Saturday night.

However, as helpful as a spoken commitment can be, that is far from being the only reason to go to a bishop. As the father of the ward, he is authorized to receive revelation in your behalf. He can give you priesthood blessings and inspired counsel. He can help you formulate a positive plan of action and use priesthood keys to assist you in your quest to repent, draw closer to the Savior, and claim the wonderful blessings of Jesus Christ's Atonement. You'll be amazed at the changes you can make when you stop relying on willpower alone and start relying on God's power.

Enlarged portraits, new backgrounds, glowing thread, micro-printing, color shifting, and watermarks that are visible in the light: these are the security features that protect us from counterfeit money. They can also be reminders of what we need to do to detect and reject Satan's counterfeit of pornography.

Brad Wilcox is an assistant professor in the Depart-ment of Teacher Education at Brigham Young Uni-versity, where he also directs the Mexico student-teaching program and Guatemala intern-ships. He served his mission in Chile and is now married with four children. He loves reading bed-time stories to his kids and also enjoys his calling as bishop of the BYU 138th Ward.

What Is the Truth?

Several years ago a young couple was anticipating the birth of another daughter. Life had been good to them. They were raising three beautiful little girls in a small Colorado town. However, during the course of this pregnancy life suddenly became more complicated. Tests were performed, and it became apparent that their infant daughter's brain wasn't developing normally. Doctors quoted facts and statistics and then explained the options to this young LDS couple, options that included terminating the developing life of their little girl. The *truth* the medical team tried to convey to this couple was that their little girl didn't have much of a chance to live a normal life. She would certainly be a drain on the family both emotionally and financially. After prayer and spending many hours with their priesthood leaders, they followed the convictions of their hearts. This growing family believed the *truth* that all life is sacred, a gift from Heavenly Father.

At the conclusion of a talk I had given about the Prophet Joseph Smith, a nonmember attending the youth conference told me how much she had enjoyed the conference and appreciated the values we hold close as members of the Church. However, she just couldn't accept Joseph Smith's testimony. She asked, "How could members of the Church accept such a story?" She continued, "The *truth* is in the Bible. There is no way God would appear to and speak with a fourteen-year-old boy in modern times."

Mike was the son of a prominent minister, the president of the Christian Medical Society at his college, and a friend of mine during medical school. Mike's lifestyle in medical school wasn't consistent with his strict, conservative, religious upbringing. He lived with two of our female classmates, drank heavily, and even experimented with illegal drugs. One afternoon during a break from school, we had an interesting conversation on a ski lift. I asked Mike if he felt guilty about living contrary to the standards with which he had been brought up. Mike told me, "The *truth* is Jesus came to the earth to save me from my sins. I don't have to feel guilty."

What is *the truth*? The Doctrine and Covenants gives us the answer. In section 93, verse 24, we read, "And truth is knowledge of things as they are, and as they were, and as they are to come." In other words, truth is a knowledge or understanding of principles, laws, or conditions that are consistent over time. They simply don't change. Another important characteristic of truth is found in verse 30: "All truth is independent in that sphere in which God has placed it." Truth is independent of our beliefs and opinions, even our hopes and desires.

I want you to try an experiment to prove my point. Take this book, hold it away from you, and then let go of it. I'll bet that it fell to the floor! Had you tried the experiment yesterday or if you were to try it tomorrow, the results would be the same. Now, hold out the book again and really believe that it won't hit the floor. Concentrate as hard as you can. Visualize the book suspended in the air. You may even want to ask a friend to believe along with you. Now let go. The book continues to fall to the ground! It doesn't matter how many people you get to believe that the book won't fall; it does fall every time. Gravity passes the test of a *true* law or principle. It remains consistent over time and isn't influenced by the beliefs or opinions of others.

In 1492 almost everyone believed that the world was flat and that if you sailed far enough into the ocean the unfortunate sailor and his boat would drop off the edge of the earth. Christopher Columbus didn't accept the opinions of the majority. He and his crew didn't fall off the edge of the earth. There was no edge. Columbus had discovered the *truth* about the world's shape. The earth had been and will continue to be round. No matter how many people believed it to be otherwise, the truth wasn't affected by their opinions.

Knowing and applying the truth in our lives is the basic foundation upon which our happiness and eternal progression must be built. Elder Dallin H. Oaks of the Quorum of the Twelve Apostles said, "Latter-day Saints should be constantly concerned with teaching and emphasizing those great and powerful eternal *truths* that will help us find our way back to the presence of our Heavenly Father" ("Powerful Ideas," *Ensign*, November 1995, p. 25).

In describing the spiritual armor critical to protecting our souls, the Lord tells us to gird or surround our loins with the truth (see D&C 27:15–16). Loins can be defined as the part of the body located between the bottom of the last rib and the hip bone. Many organs essential to our physical survival are contained within those boundaries. A significant injury to any of these organs could be fatal. Protecting our spiritual loins with a knowledge and application of the truth is just as important to our spiritual survival in our fight against Satan as protecting our mortal loins is in a physical battle.

Among the great eternal truths that will protect us here on earth and help us find our way back to the presence of our Heavenly Father are an understanding of our true relationship with our Father in Heaven, a testimony of the Prophet Joseph Smith and his role in the restoration of the gospel, and a testimony that Jesus is the Christ, the literal Son of God. All three of these principles pass the test for *truth* that we have already discussed: all are consistent over time and cannot be influenced by the beliefs or opinions of others.

You Are a Child of God

From our first days in Primary, most of us have memorized and sung the words to "I Am a Child of God." I don't know that many of us understand the eternal significance of these lyrics.

From the first chapter of Moses in the Pearl of Great Price, it is clear that our relationship with our Father is a truth of particular importance to Him. In a vision opened to Moses, the Lord speaks with His prophet face to face. After the Lord identifies Himself in verse 3, the first *truth* that He teaches His young prophet is that

Moses is literally a son of God. The lesson is so important that the Lord repeats it three different times (see verses 4, 6, and 7). Just a few verses later we can see the importance of understanding and applying this truth when "Satan came tempting him" (verse 12). Moses, armed with the understanding that he was literally a spirit son of God, then had the power to resist the temptations of Satan.

When you find yourself at the checkout counter at a video-rental store with an inappropriate movie, does the knowledge of your true relationship with Him give rise to a voice in your heart which says, "I am a child of God. I know who I am and what is expected of me"? If you find yourself in an uncomfortable situation on a date, does that same truth whisper to your mind, "Teach me all that I must do to live with Him someday?" The young LDS couple I described earlier understood their relationship with their Heavenly Father and their yet-unborn daughter. Father was sending one of His precious little girls to their family. That *truth* led them to the decision to lovingly care for and nurture their little baby, no matter what her physical problems would be. They appropriately named her Sonny. She was a beautiful and content little girl who brought a great deal of joy to family and friends alike for several months until she returned home to her Father. While there was sadness when Sonny passed away, the knowledge that her Father had taken her home became a source of strength and peace to this young family. There will come into your life a great power as you make similar decisions based on your true relationship with Father. We are His children; that will never change and could never be influenced by the beliefs and opinions of others.

Joseph the Prophet

On a beautiful spring morning in 1820, a young teenage boy went into a grove of trees near Palmyra, New York. The young man was confused about religion and went to pray to his Father in Heaven for an answer. In response to that prayer, God the Father and His Son, Jesus Christ, appeared to the young man Joseph Smith. That single truth has changed the lives of millions throughout the world. However, if everyone alive were to disbelieve and mock the testimony of the Prophet, it could not change the fact that God indeed appeared to Joseph that morning. It really doesn't matter what you and I think or believe, because the truth is completely independent of our opinions. Joseph Smith saw and spoke with God. It is simply the truth. Having discovered that truth, we should then apply the principles that the Prophet Joseph taught. One particular lesson that has impressed me was the forgiving nature of Joseph Smith.

W. W. Phelps was a convert to the Church. He started out faithful to the Prophet and worked hard as a printer for the new church. After some difficulty of his own, Brother Phelps became disillusioned and rebelled openly against the Prophet. He eventually became a principal source of great suffering to the early members of the Church. The years passed and the suffering was endured. Having repented, Brother Phelps asked Joseph to forgive him and accept him back into fellowship in the Church. The Prophet's response further exemplifies the truth of his mission: "It is true, that we have suffered much in consequence of your behavior—the cup of gall, already full enough . . . , was indeed filled to overflowing when you turned against us. . . . However, the cup has been drunk, the will of our Father has been done, and we are yet alive . . . . Believing your confession to be real, and your repentance genuine, I shall be happy once again to give you the right hand of fellowship. . . . Come on, dear brother, since the war is past, for friends at first, are friends again at last" (*History of the Church*, 4:163–64).

Do you want to know the truth about what Joseph Smith said he saw and heard? Follow the principles he taught, and you will know the truth. The Church's current President stands as the Lord's prophet and literal successor to the Prophet Joseph. He teaches the same truth that Joseph taught. While our testimony neither adds to nor detracts from the divinity and truthfulness of his calling, it certainly acts as our own personal anchor against the storms of temptation and confusion we face in the world today.

Jesus Is the Christ

In a world that is increasingly engrossed by the need to have scientific explanations of why things work, the simple truths of the gospel are easily dismissed by the so-called wise. We are literally living the fulfillment of a Book of Mormon prophecy: "By very small means the Lord doth confound the wise and bringeth about the salvation of many souls" (Alma 37:7). Despite the elaborate theories that many scientists use to explain the creation of the earth, they are only the opinions of men, which have definitely changed with time. The *truth* is that the Savior, under the direction of His Father, created the world (see John 1:1–3).

His work wasn't finished with the Creation. Our Father in Heaven understood that sin, or making mistakes, would be a condition of our eternal progression. Knowing that all of us would fall short of the perfection required to return to our heavenly home, Jesus voluntarily offered to atone for those sins. Many laugh at the idea of a Savior and also deny the existence of God. Their beliefs and opinions will never change the *truths* that God does indeed live and that the love of the Savior makes it possible for all of us to return to the presence of our Father in Heaven.

Jesus taught us a valuable technique to discover truth: "By their fruits ye shall know them" (Matthew 7:20). In other words, if you want to know if a man speaks the truth and is who he says he is, look at his life and the results of how he lives his life. The fruits of the Savior's life are sweet and filling.

It had been a busy day for Jesus, filled with healing, comforting, and teaching. He was undoubtedly tired as He quickly passed through the city of Nain surrounded by followers. Given the events of the day, was it any wonder that so many had questions and wanted to be near Him? At the city gate, the Savior and His followers noticed a funeral procession. Moved by the sight, Jesus must have inquired about the solemn event. A widowed mother was burying her only son. The Savior maneuvered through the crowd and asked that the procession stop. He approached the bier and spoke to the lifeless body: "Young man, I say unto thee, Arise" (Luke 7:14). Jesus didn't then quickly move on, but He took the time to deliver the son to his mother. Though preoccupied and probably tired, the Savior took the time to love and serve others. How well do we apply the simple truth that He taught us by his own example? Remember, truth remains consistent over time. In 1832 the Lord revealed the same truth to the Prophet Joseph Smith: "Succor the weak, lift up the hands which hang down, and strengthen the feeble knees" (D&C 81:5).

Every mission has at least one missionary with a mission-wide reputation. On my mission, I received a transfer letter, and my new companion was just that kind of elder. Numerous jokes circulated through the mission based on how he dressed, how he spoke, and many other personality quirks. Although I had never met this elder, I had heard the stories from other missionaries and I didn't want to know him. For a week I dreaded the transfer. I tried to figure out what it was that I had done to deserve such a fate. My companions teased and assured me that after working with this elder I would never be the same; he would certainly rub off on me.

Reluctantly I made the move, and unfortunately I found out that my new companion was everything I feared. The elder wore his pants too high, his Spanish accent was irritating, he didn't know the discussions very well, his acne was a real attention getter, and his hair always looked greasy. After we had been together for a couple of weeks, our relationship hadn't progressed past being mere acquaintances.

Walking back to our apartment in a town just west of Mexico City one evening, there was some obvious tension between us. My companion broke the silence and said, "You were disappointed with the transfer." I didn't know how to respond. He continued, "You now know that I'm just as weird as everyone in the mission says I am." How could he know what everyone in the mission was saying? I'm sure that no one had told him face-to-face what missionaries whispered after district meetings. I mumbled the obligatory "Of course not, Elder." He turned away and said, "Elder, your actions betray your thoughts."

His statement was right on target. While I hadn't teased him about the personal quirks that made him strange to many in the mission, I had done little to serve him. Certainly his hands hung down, and I did nothing to lift them. His knees were feeble, and I made no attempt to strengthen them. I realized that night that he was the way he was because none of his companions had ever followed the example of the Savior in serving.

This same scenario is played out in almost every high school in North America and unfortunately it is also the case in many families. I promise you that if you will follow the example of the Savior and taste this particular fruit, you will know that Jesus is the Son of God and that He taught eternal truth that will lead us back into His presence.

When you know the truth, life is not confusing. Difficulties and challenges will still come our way. Decisions will still have to be made. When we make those decisions based on principles that remain consistent over time, principles that cannot be influenced by the opinion and beliefs of others, we will certainly find our way back home to Father. That is the truth!

Curtis Galke is an emergency room physician in southern Illinois. After graduating from Brigham Young University, he attended medical school in California and then completed a three-year family practice residency with the U.S. Air Force. Upon completion of his residency, Curt and his family lived for three years in Panama, where he worked as a flight surgeon. The highlights of his life include  *flying in an F-16, playing the Tabernacle organ, serving a mission to Mexico City, marriage to his wife, Alethea, and playing with his four active boys.*

A Profile of Courage

My wife, Bess Angell, was named for a great woman. When Angell's great-grandmother was to be given a name and a father's blessing, her father, George Edward Angell, thought he had the last word in the situation. He and his wife had not been able to agree on the name for their daughter. Since he was the one giving her a name and a blessing, he figured that he would give her the name he liked. He walked boldly to the front of the chapel and gave his daughter his favorite name: Rebecca Ann. Feeling good about it, he walked back down the aisle to sit by his wife. She did not feel good about it! She said, softly but firmly, "I will never call her that!" She never did. Her favorite name was Bess. Their daughter was called Bess by her mother and Rebecca Ann by her father her entire life. My wife and her cousin were both named for her: her cousin was named Rebecca Ann and my wife was named Bess Angell. I am grateful that my wife's parents chose to name her the favorite name of her great-great-grandmother and not her great-great-grandfather, because I am one of the few men who can say that I am ministered to by an angel every day!

Walking toward the front of the chapel with my newborn son to give him a name and a blessing, I was grateful that Angell and I had agreed on the same name for him. Soon this little son would have recorded on the records of the Church the single name he would hear more than any other for the rest of his life. It would become the way to identify him, his personal calling card, his very own name. We named him Jonathan Ruel for both of his grandfathers, both great men. We had already named our first daughter for both of her grandmothers, so it seemed appropriate. We felt as Helaman did as he selected names for his sons. He explained to his sons the reasons for choosing to name them Nephi and Lehi: "Behold, I have given unto you the names of our first parents who came out of the land of Jerusalem; and this I have done that when you remember your names ye may remember them; and when ye remember them ye may remember their works; and when ye remember their works ye may know how that it is said, and also written, that they were good. Therefore, my sons, I would that ye should do that which is good, that it may be said of you, and also written, even as it has been said and written of them" (Helaman 5:6–7).

If you were to come to our home, we would show you our hall of fame. Displayed on the walls in the hall are framed pictures of our children. At the base of each picture is an additional frame displaying the child's name and its meaning along with a scripture that represents their name. For example, our seven-year-old is named Jenali. Her name means "sent from God as a gift." She brought a lot of joy and peace with her, and so we selected 3 Nephi 12:9 to represent her name: "Blessed are all the peacemakers, for they shall be called the children of God." Jenali is not yet always a peacemaker—just ask her brothers, who she loves to tease—but she knows that her Heavenly Father wants her to be one. Her name is an inspiration to help her become more Christlike each day.

Selecting just the right name has been challenging enough for us that two of our children left the hospital with birth certificates that said "Baby Anderson" because we just hadn't found the perfect name yet. In contemplating the naming process, we like to think about what the prophet Mormon's feelings might have been as he named his son Moroni. Put yourself in his place for a moment. Mormon lived in a time when wickedness was everywhere. He knew that this boy would have to be strong and courageous. He knew that this son would often stand alone for what was right and that his name would be known for many generations to come. We like to think that Mormon wanted to give his son a name that would inspire him, just as Helaman had wanted his sons to be inspired by the names he had chosen for them. We can imagine Mormon searching the historical record to find an incredible mortal example of courage, strength, and faith so that his son might share this identity. Such a man was Captain Moroni. Of him, Mormon himself wrote: "If all men had been, and were, and ever would be, like unto Moroni, behold, the very powers of hell would have been shaken forever; yea, the devil would never have power over the hearts of the children of men" (Alma 48:17).

This wonderful tribute to Moroni was passed on as a legacy of courage to Mormon's incredible son and to us. Since these latter days are also times when we often have to stand courageously and alone for the things that are right, what can we learn from Captain Moroni to help keep Satan out of our lives? Let's look at some of the attributes that contributed to Captain Moroni's courage.

Perfect Understanding

The scriptures say "Moroni was a strong and a mighty man; he was a man of a perfect understanding" (Alma 48:11).

Look at the footnote for this scripture, which leads us to Alma 18:22. At this point in the account of Ammon and King Lamoni in the land of Ishmael, Ammon had already become the king's servant, gathered the scattered flocks of the king, slain the enemy with stones and "disarmed" them, carried the arms to the king, astounded the king and his entire court, perceived the thoughts of the king, explained that he was not the Great Spirit, and been told by the king that whatsoever he desired of the king he would grant it to him. Whew! Then in verse 22 we read, "Now Ammon being wise, yet harmless, he said unto Lamoni: Wilt thou hearken unto my words, if I tell thee by what power I do these things? And this is the thing that I desire of thee." Ammon was being led by the Spirit to know what to say to the king. He knew the king would give him anything he had. Anything! But he listened to the spirit to know exactly what to ask for. Ammon knew that if the king would listen to the gospel, be influenced by the Spirit, and become converted, that his household and many of his people would follow suit and an entire group of people would have a change of heart! That is exactly what happened. In fact, they had no more desire to do evil, became a righteous people, and established the Church among them.

The spiritual discernment Ammon possessed was the same attribute Captain Moroni possessed with his "perfect understanding." In Alma 48:18 we read, "Behold, he was a man like unto Ammon, the son of Mosiah, yea, and even the other sons of Mosiah, yea, and also Alma and his sons, for they were all men of God."

Michael Stevenson was a young man who loved to surf, enjoy life, and read. He would read each night, and as he would finish a book he would come to his mother and say, "That was a good book, but I want a better book!" She finally tired of the request and handed young Michael the Bible and said it was the best book of all. For the next several years, Michael studied the contents of the Bible carefully and, blessed with spiritual discernment, he began making a list of unexplainable statements made in the Bible. These statements became a list of questions that no one seemed to be able to answer. The list included:

Why were there always prophets that led God's people, but we don't have one today?

Where is the stick of Joseph? The stick of Judah is the Bible, but where is its companion?

What is the principle of baptism for the dead?

Why don't we have Apostles today like they did in the days of the Savior?

As Michael grew older, he fell in love with a beautiful young woman. After they were married, he added questions to his list, such as: I love Jenny so much, how could it possibly be that after this life I would not feel anything more for her than I would for anyone else? How could it be heaven without her?

The list became pages of typed, single-spaced questions that kept pushing Michael to search for answers. After graduation from college, Michael signed up for the navy. He was told that he could travel and see exotic ports. He had a chance to list his top five places to be assigned. He listed places in Europe and the Pacific, but he ended up in New Mexico in the desert. His office had four people in it. One was the president and another the executive secretary in the local branch of the Church.

Not long after Michael's arrival, everyone from the office was reassigned elsewhere for a week except the branch president and

Michael. On Tuesday morning of that week, during a moment when they were sharing small talk, the branch president mentioned that his family had been to the movies for family home evening the night before. He mentioned that the movie had been about aliens. Michael thought, *I knew the Mormons had something to do with aliens!* He hesitated to ask, but since they were alone he mustered the courage and tentatively said, "Do the Mormons believe in life on other planets?" The branch president began to explain the entire plan of salvation, including where we came from, why we are here, and where we are going. After two and a half hours of explanation, the branch president said, "So I guess we do believe in life in other places."

Michael was enthralled. He started to ask more questions. As the day wore on, they talked of nothing else. At quitting time, Michael stood at the door and wouldn't let the branch president leave until he heard more. On Friday night, Michael blocked the doorway one more time, pleading, "Just teach me a little more." The branch president explained, "I have taught you about everything I know!" He then said, "Michael, you need to see the missionaries and hear the basic principles of the gospel clearly explained in an organized way." Michael agreed. As Michael left the office, he thought of his list of questions about the Bible and realized that without ever having brought up his list or having intentionally asked the questions, he had received answers to every one of the questions on his list!

Michael's search was long and hard. The Spirit guided him from the time he was young to search for the truth. When the missionaries came to his home, he let them in, shut the door, and said, "You can't leave until we have received all the lessons you have." After the Stevensons' baptism and beautiful marriage in the temple, they are now sharing this beautiful message with others as much as they can. And the happiness they radiate is amazing. They are a great example of the power of the guidance of the Spirit, which leads us to a perfect understanding.

Service

The scriptures say, "Moroni was . . . a man whose soul did joy in the liberty and the freedom of his country, and his brethren . . . a man who did labor exceedingly for the welfare and safety of his people" (Alma 48:11–12).

John's junior year was almost complete, and he was looking forward to the opportunity to spend the summer working and preparing for his senior football season. He had been playing for many years, and this would be the final chance to prepare for a college football contract, his big dream. How could he possibly complicate his plans by running for a student-body office? Why would the adviser ask him to run regardless of the demands on his time, and who would vote for him, anyway? It all seemed so confusing. He made the decision to run for office.

After a couple of phone calls, he had a campaign manager and other friends who would be a support. The plans were underway. There was the speech, and the posters, and calling most of the school to seek their support. Suddenly the primary election was over, and he was in the final election. The night before the big assembly during which his skit was to be presented, he came home to find that his brother, who had taken his dogs for a walk, seemed to have been gone for a very long time. A search began. As the night wore on, the concern increased and a desperate family frantically combed the hills. They found no trace or clue. John returned home long enough the next morning to eat and change his clothes and call his friends. "I'm so sorry," he said. "I know how much work you have put into my campaign, but you will just have to take my name out of the race. Finding my brother is more important." His brother was never found, and the search finally concluded.

John was elected student-body president without being there for his skit or the election. He returned to find himself summoned into a meeting where the beginning plans for the next year were unfolding. The first matters of business seemed to revolve around parties for the new officers, the sweaters they would wear, and things such as that. It just hit him wrong, and he announced that maybe he had better resign. The others struggled to understand. "I decided to do this because I thought that perhaps we could help others, but all we are doing is helping ourselves," he explained. "What if we took some of the money we would use on ourselves and made a charitable fund? We could use it to get a little something for kids in the school who might be in special need." They established a fund, but the amount set aside for the entire year was depleted by the end of September. John's high school had so many students facing challenging circumstances that the need was tremendous.

Without anyone knowing, John picked up a part-time job and put his paychecks in the fund. At the end of the year, the audit showed that many times the budgeted amount had been spent on students in need. Finally John confessed quietly to his adviser that he had been stuffing the fund all year with his own money. He had been busy with football, school, student-body office, and trying to do it all well enough that he might qualify for a university scholarship, but he had still quietly found a way to keep the fund afloat.

Earlier that school year, during October, he received a phone call at home one evening. A shy female voice said, "Is this President John?" He answered, "Please just call me John." "But you are the president of the high school, right?" she asked. Then came the request. "I am a tenth-grade girl at your school, and we have a girl's-choice dance coming up." It was coming all right, but not until February, over four months away. "I just wondered," she continued. "if you would go to the dance with me?" He quickly accepted and then said, "I hope to see you at school. Maybe we could get to know each other better." "That would be easy," she said. "I know where all your classes are!"

John didn't think much about what might happen until a week later in the locker room as he was getting ready for the football game.

Another player asked him how it felt to have a date four months ahead of time. He asked his friend how he could possibly know about that, and he explained that the sophomore was his sister's best friend. John made one simple request: "You can say anything to me that you want, but just leave her alone." His friend then asked, "Why do you care? You don't even know her." He answered, "Does that matter?"

The months came and went, and February finally arrived. The girls at the school were in charge of the activities. They were planning a donkey-style basketball game the night before the dance to raise money for an orphanage. John was going to MC the event. He hurried home after school, and things seemed very quiet. He looked through the house and found it empty, and then he stepped into the study and found that a tragedy had happened in his family. His father was dead. Just then his mom pulled up in front of the house with the car filled with the kids.

At 7:30 the game was to begin and John hadn't shown up, so they were preparing to start without him when the door swung open and in came John. He conducted most of the fun and games. Afterward he spent a sleepless night and then a busy, emotional day taking care of family and details. That night was the girls' dance. The last thing he felt like doing was going on a date with someone he didn't know and trying to show her a good time. However, at 6:30 he was at her house with flowers in hand, and they had a wonderful evening. About 11:00 she mentioned to John that he seemed quiet and she wondered if everything was all right. He was afraid that she might take his lack of enthusiasm personally, so for the first time he described what had been happening. He hadn't mentioned it before because he didn't want to spoil her evening. I don't doubt for a minute that there are many of you out there who are much like this, who have learned to serve even in difficult circumstances. Thank you for your willingness to serve; you don't know how many are influenced by your example.

Gratitude

The description of Captain Moroni continues: "A man whose heart did swell with thanksgiving to his God, for the many privileges and blessings which he bestowed upon his people" (Alma 48:12).

Thaila had spent a busy day dancing as a member of the cast for the school play. What an all-day workout! She just had time to run home and get ready for a busy evening. She was moving to music in her car when pain suddenly hit. Then she found she couldn't move her arms. The car headed for the curb. She stopped but could not use her arms to steer or turn off the car. Finally a passerby stopped, and through tears Thalia explained the pain she was feeling and her inability to move.

By the time she was in the hospital, her legs were numb too. Her wonderful father gave her a blessing. She was told in the blessing that through her faith and the faith of her friends she would be made whole. Her friends heard about this blessing and suggested having a fast for her. As I remember, about 180 students crowded into a seminary room at the end of the school day. After a day of fasting, I met with them to have a prayer. Her brother led her wonderful friends in the prayer. I remember him saying, "She is an angel on earth, Father, and she deserves to have this blessing fulfilled. Please allow her to be able to move her arms and legs again."

A few days following this prayer, I was busy at my desk early one morning when I heard happy laughter coming down the hall. I looked up and saw Thalia coming toward me with arms and legs all working perfectly again. I hurried into the hall to greet her, and she spun me around and said, "Guess what!" I replied, "I think I know what." She oozed with enthusiasm as she showed me that her arms and legs were working again. Then she explained that something unusual had happened in the hospital: her fingers had been connected to her tear ducts. I was a little puzzled, so I asked for an explanation. She went on, "Every morning when I get up, I hold up my hands so I can see them, and then I move my fingers and the tears start. Then I move my toes, and there are more tears." She said she used to find herself wishing that she could lose five pounds or change her hair. Now she just smiled as she watched her hand pick up her toothbrush and brush her own teeth and pick up her brush and brush her own hair. "I have never felt this happy," she said. "It is so great to just be alive!"

This new exuberance for life put her in some interesting circumstances. During the subsequent summer she went to Europe with her grandmother. While they were touring London, she climbed the stairs of a double-deck bus. As she reached the top she was beaming with radiance because her own legs had just climbed the stairs. *Certainly there must be some Olympic honor for this,* she thought. A young couple from Canada was sitting at the back of the bus enjoying their honeymoon in Europe. Even though couples on their honeymoon don't usually pay attention to anyone except each other, they couldn't help but notice the radiant, dark-haired girl at the front of the bus. They were so intrigued by her that they came up from the back of the bus just to ask what made her so happy. She said, "My arms move and my legs move!" They said, "Well, ours do too, but we don't seem to be quite as happy as you." She replied, "Mine didn't used to, but there is another reason. It's because I know there is a purpose to life, and I'll bet you wish you knew what it was too!" They spent the remainder of the ride around London, dinner that night, and breakfast the next morning talking about the gospel. As they were leaving to go and get on the plane, she explained that she had a couple of friends who lived in their town, that their names were Elder and Elder, and that they would love to come over and tell them more.

The next fall after school had just started, Thalia bounced in my office early one morning. She was so happy. She shared the phone call she had received from Canada. The couple on the bus had called to tell her they were just as happy as she was because they had just been baptized. Thalia bubbled over as she said, "Do you know how that makes me feel? I am going to go find someone else to talk to!"

Faith

Captain Moroni "was a man who was firm in the faith of Christ, and he had sworn with an oath to defend his people, his rights, and his country, and his religion, even to the loss of his blood" (Alma 48:13). By the way, he was only fifteen.

It was 3:30 A.M., and I had been awakened in bed. I had been a bishop for only ten hours. The Spirit was quietly but directly whispering to me that I had a young man in my ward who needed me. I felt clearly and deeply a great love for this young man and a great need to reach out to him and tell him how much his Heavenly Father loved him and wanted to help him.

As he came into the bishop's office some hours later, he immediately began to cry. We prayed, and he freely confessed a very serious sin. We shared scriptures together, cried together, and prayed again. I tried to tell him how much the Lord loved him. He said, "I don't believe you." It shocked me. He then asked, "How can the Lord love me now, with what I have done?" I tried to explain that the Lord loves us because He is good, not because we are. I showed him scriptural references confirming this. He still wouldn't believe me.

The process of repentance was not easy. Some time later he came into my office on a Sunday morning. He said he was getting answers to his prayers again. We prayed together and felt that it was time for him to take the sacrament again. He felt that he was ready. As the sacrament meeting began, he sat quietly in the back corner of the chapel. As the sacrament was blessed, a young priest recited those amazing words, "O God, the Eternal Father, we ask thee in the name of thy Son, Jesus Christ, to bless and sanctify . . ." (D&C 20:77). I am not certain that many priests understand what sanctify means or that this priest knew that his priesthood would be the sacred vehicle that would help heal someone so much in need. A deacon took the tray to the back row. Our eyes met as he prepared to take the sacrament for the first time in a long time. He quietly bowed his head and as he later told me, pleadingly prayed, "Please forgive me and allow me to renew my covenants with thee."

Even from the front of the chapel I could tell that the Atonement was working a miracle in the back of the chapel. He was feeling the love that I had felt from the Lord for him. He was feeling cleansed and forgiven. He came to me after the meeting and asked if we could go into the office. I followed him in, and before I knew it, he was on his knees. I knelt by him as he poured out his gratitude to his Heavenly Father for the love that he felt so freely and for this wonderful cleansing power of the Atonement. He quietly said, "This is the happiest day of my life!"

He went on a mission some time after this experience. About six months later I received a letter that said, "When I told you that it was the happiest day in my life, I was wrong. Today has been the happiest day. I baptized six people today, and as I brought the father out of the water and looked up at his sweet family, all dressed in white and so filled with love for each other and for our Heavenly Father and His Son, it was amazing. Having it yourself is great, but giving this joy to someone else is even better." He served a wonderful mission, then returned home.

Some time later, he was preparing to be married in the temple to a beautiful young woman. As we met in the temple, I had a quiet moment with him and shared with him as I shook his hand that I knew his hand was clean and prepared for this sacred ordinance. He agreed. I asked if he remembered why it was clean, and he said he did. I asked how much he loved our Heavenly Father and His Son. He shared with me his testimony. I asked if he would do me a favor, then I requested, "When you kneel at the altar, quietly look in your sweetheart's eyes and ask, How much does the Lord love me?" As he knelt I witnessed his tears as the Spirit once again confirmed the Lord's love to a wonderful young man. He said after the ceremony, "This is the happiest day in my life. My companions in the mission field were great, but nothing like this!"

More time passed, and soon he was standing at the front of a chapel with his hands wrapped around his beautiful baby. After the name and a blessing were conferred, he held up the baby as if to say, "Don't we look a lot alike?" Then he quietly said to me, "This is my happiest day!"

Helaman selected *Nephi* and *Lehi* as names for his sons to help them remember to be Christlike. Mormon named his son Moroni, and certainly it inspired Moroni to have understanding and courage and live a life of Christlike service. As members of The Church of Jesus Christ of Latter-day Saints, we have the privilege and blessing at baptism to take upon us the name of Jesus Christ. Each week as we partake of the sacrament, we have the sacred opportunity to renew our baptismal covenants. We can have His Spirit with us by keeping our covenant to "always remember him and keep his com-mandments which he has given" (D&C 20:77). By putting Him first in our lives, we will remember what He wants us to do, and not be influenced by what the world wants us to do. I testify that He lives and that He loves us, and that "there shall be no other name given . . . whereby salvation can come unto the children of men, only in and through the name of Christ" (Mosiah 3:17).

Scott Anderson and his wife, Angell, live in Bluff-dale, Utah, where they spend time working on home improvement projects, waiting for their children to come to family meetings, and ordering pizza as a reward for cleaning the house. He likes to travel, and his favorite places to go are New Jersey and Georgia to see his married children and darling grandchildren. His hobbies include teaching, writ-ing, music, enjoying the outdoors, sports, and building memories with his family. He has a Ph.D. in marriage and family therapy from BYU and is currently on the faculty at the Orem Institute of Religion adjacent to Utah Valley State College. When asked to describe his personality, his wife says that he is a "gratitude guru" and a "life enthusiast" who loves to serve.

Drink and Never Thirst

Have you ever thought much about the pitcher of water that always seems to be sitting on the stand or podium of a speaker? You know, the one that is ice cold and has droplets of condensation rolling gently down the sides, the one that they rarely use and that we listeners usually wish we had access to!

Water is so important in our lives. I would like to share a few interesting facts I have found about water.

- Water covers seventy percent of the earth's surface.
- Without water there can be no life. Every living thing, including plants, animals, and humans must have water to exist.
- Your body is two-thirds, or sixty-five percent, water.
- On average a person takes in about 16,000 gallons of water during his or her lifetime.
- Every glass of water you drink contains molecules of water used countless times before.
- Humans can live without food for more than a month, but they can live without water for only a week.
- If your body loses more than twenty percent of its normal water content, it will die painfully.
- A human must take in about two and a half quarts of water a day. It may be in the form of drinks, water itself, or water in food.
- Doctors comment that if patients would drink eight to ten glasses of water a day, they wouldn't need to see about seventy percent of them.

- Some urologists say they stay in business because people choose soda pop and carbonated drinks over drinking water.
- Water flushes the body of toxins and impurities and helps keep the body pure and clean.

Water is literally the lifeblood of our physical bodies. We would die without its constant intake.

Just as our physical bodies need water, so do our spiritual bodies. The Lord told Isaiah, "Every one that thirsteth, come ye to the waters" (Isaiah 55:1). Nephi said, "Come, my brethren, every one that thirsteth, come ye to the waters" (2 Nephi 9:50). The Lord told John the Revelator, "I will give unto him that is athirst of the fountain of the water of life freely" (Revelation 21:6). And John recorded, "In the last day, that great day of the feast, Jesus stood and cried, saying, If any man thirst, let him come unto me, and drink" (John 7:37).

What is this spiritual water which is made mention of so many times? It is Jesus Christ and His teachings. We learn of Him and His commandments through reading the scriptures. He is that living water which will sustain our eternal spirits.

Probably one of the greatest stories of living water is found in John 4:1–30. It is the story of Jesus at the well with a woman of Samaria. Jesus and his disciples had just left Judaea and were headed for Galilee. The shortest way to Galilee was through an area called Samaria. The problem, however, was a longtime dislike and even hatred between the two peoples. Jews felt that the Samaritans were beneath them because the Samaritans were a mixed people, in whom the blood of Israel was mingled with that of the Assyrians and other nations, and also because the Samaritans accepted only part of the scriptures. Jews would literally do anything in their power to avoid them. But Jesus had instructed the disciples to travel through Samaria, and so they obeyed.

As they approached Samaria, they stopped by a well called Jacob's well. Jesus sat down and requested his disciples to go into the city and buy food. A woman of Samaria came to the well to draw water, and Jesus said to her, "Give me to drink." The custom of that time was to never refuse anyone who asked you for water. But the woman was taken aback because it was also a custom for men not to speak to strange women, and not only was she a stranger but a Samaritan.

She quickly responded by saying, "How is it that thou, being a Jew, askest drink of me, which am a woman of Samaria? for the Jews have no dealings with the Samaritans."

Jesus answered, "If thou knewest the gift of God, and who it is that saith to thee, Give me to drink; thou wouldest have asked of him, and he would have given thee living water."

The woman was puzzled by this statement. She could see that He had no vessel with which to obtain water, and yet he talked of giving her living water. When she inquired further, He said, "Whosoever drinketh of this water [making reference to the well] shall thirst again: But whosoever drinketh of the water that I shall give him shall never thirst; but the water that I shall give him shall be in him a well of water springing up into everlasting life."

With much interest, and believing that Jesus was making reference to some magical water which would satisfy her physical thirst, she said, "Give me this water, that I thirst not, neither come hither to draw."

Seeing her confusion, Jesus began to ask her about her husband. He then proceeded to tell her about her personal life. She knew at once that He was special and said, "I perceive that thou art a prophet."

After Christ had briefly prophesied to her, she said, "I know that Messias cometh, which is called Christ: when he is come, he will tell us all things."

Then, at one of the few times that Christ ever directly revealed His divine mission, He said, "I that speak unto thee am he."

Christ indeed is that living water to which He made reference to the woman at the well. It is only through Him that we can know the fullness of eternal life and satisfy our spiritual thirst. So how is it possible, we may ask ourselves, to draw closer and learn of Him?

Jesus taught the Pharisees, who literally and wrongly worshiped the scriptures, how to learn of Him. The Pharisees didn't understand that the scriptures themselves did not bring them eternal life but were the vehicle that brought them to Christ, who in turn gives eternal life. The Savior corrected them when he said they "search the scriptures; for in them ye think ye have eternal life: and they are they which testify of me. And ye will not come to me, that ye might have life" (John 5:39–40).

Unlike the Pharisees, we should read the scriptures with the intent of coming to Christ. And just as our physical bodies need water on a daily basis or they will perish, we must drink from the scriptures daily or our spiritual well-being could become weak and perish also.

Reading the scriptures seems like such an easy thing to do, and yet it can be difficult, especially if we are not in tune with the Spirit. Even prophets sometimes struggle with their spirituality. President Kimball said, "I find that when I get casual in my relationships with divinity and when it seems that no divine ear is listening and no divine voice is speaking, that I am far, far away. If I immerse myself in the scriptures the distance narrows and the spirituality returns" (Edward L. Kimball, ed., *The Teachings of Spencer W. Kimball* [Salt Lake City: Bookcraft, 1982], p. 135).

It is easy to drink physical water daily, but how do we manage to read our scriptures daily? We may sometimes feel that if we just load up with our reading on Sunday, it will last us for the week. But just as loading ourselves up with water once a week doesn't work—unless, of course, we are a camel—neither will a once-a-week reading. We must sup from the scriptures daily.

Let me share with you a great spiritual awakening concerning the scriptures that happened in my life. I was fortunate enough to be born into the Church and have been an active member all my life. I have tried to attend my meetings, obey the commandments, and occasionally read my scriptures when time permitted. The only problem was, time just didn't permit it very often. You see, I was much too busy! You know the problem, don't you?

As a teenager and college student, I was involved with school, sports, dating, and of course Church activities, and there just wasn't enough time to read my scriptures daily.

The problem didn't change when I got married and had children. I was too busy being a wife and mother, cooking, cleaning, and doing my Church work to read my scriptures daily. However, I did have the time every day at one o'clock to fold diapers or clean the kitchen while the TV was on. And I did manage to watch the ten o'clock news and M*A*S*H every night. After all, I deserved it. That was my reward and means of relaxation after a hard day.

Now, understand that I never sat down for a whole hour and watched that one particular program at one o'clock. I was too busy for that! But I did manage to make sure that I was at home during that time. I can even remember coming home early from daytime Relief Society homemaking activities to, uh, fold diapers and do dishes.

I know, I know! Now you are thinking that I was hooked on that program, aren't you? Well, I wasn't! I just needed to be at home at that time in order to fulfill my homemaking duties.

Yeah, right! Who was I kidding? I was gone hook, line, and sinker. I never seemed to have time to read my scriptures daily, but I always had time to fold diapers at one o'clock.

Then it happened. One day my television just blew up! I personally think that God zapped it. Suddenly I began having withdrawal symptoms every day at one o'clock. What was happening in Rachel's life? Did Mac find out that the baby wasn't really his?

Can you believe it? I was consumed with a fictitious story about fictitious people that didn't even exist. I was seriously worried about something that was totally unreal.

Now I was faced with a dilemma. What was I going to do at one o'clock and at bedtime? With my TV gone, I had nothing to do. I actually had time on my hands. So, to borrow an old advertising phrase, I let my fingers do the walking, but not through the Yellow Pages, through my scriptures.

I couldn't believe the change that began to occur in my life. Now, instead of reading fictitious stories about fictitious people, I was reading about real people like you and me who had real problems, turned to the Lord for help, and overcame them. I read stories about Christ and His example and teachings. I began to develop a spiritual thirst, if you will, for my scriptures. What once seemed not so palatable now became a delicious well of thirst-quenching spiritual water from which I looked forward to partaking daily.

As a result of this event in my life, I also noticed a new spiritual awakening and found myself thinking more about Christ. I felt as though I knew Him and wanted to be more like Him. My testimony and understanding of the gospel grew and deepened. I became more spiritually in tune. How grateful I am for the tragic death of my TV. By the way, we didn't fix the TV for sixteen years. Yep folks, that's right! No TV for sixteen years!

Some time ago I went to my bishop for a temple recommend, and we discussed the importance of the proper wearing of our temple garments. He gave me a copy of an *Ensign* article by Elder Carlos E. Asay of the Seventy. I found the introduction most interesting:

"A few years ago, in a seminar for new temple presidents and matrons, Elder James E. Faust, then of the Quorum of the Twelve Apostles, told about his being called to serve as a General Authority. He was asked only one question by President Harold B. Lee: 'Do you wear the garments properly?' to which he answered in the affirmative. He then asked if President Lee wasn't going to ask him about his worthiness. President Lee replied that he didn't need to, for he had learned from experience that how one wears the garment is the expression of how the individual feels about the Church and everything that relates to it. It is a measure of one's worthiness and devotion to the gospel" ("The Temple Garment: 'An Outward Expression of an Inward Commitment,'" *Ensign*, August 1997, p. 19).

Just as proper wearing of the garments by endowed members reflects one's worthiness and devotion to the gospel, so do the reading and studying of the scriptures. If we read and study daily, we will be drinking of spiritual waters. Our lives will focus on Christ, and we will have power to resist the temptations of the adversary.

It is my prayer that you will somehow reclaim the time necessary to drink daily from the pages of the scriptures. I also pray that you will experience the peace and tranquillity that comes from having Christ, the living water, at the center of your life.

Vivian R. Cline was born and raised in Atlanta, Georgia, and attended BYU, majoring in clothing and textiles. She is an international skin care and figure consultant and former Mrs. Utah America. As an author and professional speaker she has recently copyrighted her own "Executive Home Management System" for women and shares with them the tools necessary to become successful  *homemakers. She is the wife of S. Douglas Cline and the mother of three returned missionary sons and two beautiful teenage daughters.*

Waiting upon the Lord

*"But they that wait upon the Lord shall renew their strength;
they shall mount up with wings as eagles; they shall run, and
not be weary; and they shall walk, and not faint."*
—ISAIAH 40:31

As I visit with youth throughout the Church, you often share some of your most heartfelt desires with me. I see your challenges and pain in situations that you wish would be resolved. These problems seem to fall into two main categories. The first category includes situations that can be resolved through the use of agency, either yours or someone else's. Examples that fall in this category include: desiring that a loved one join the Church, wishing your parents wouldn't get divorced, or fitting in with a certain group of kids at school. The second category deals with situations in which agency isn't an issue. These things can't be resolved simply by someone making a different choice. Some longings in this category include wishing you could grow five inches in the next year so that you can make the basketball team, praying that your home will be protected from an impending tornado (I heard that one in Texas), or being healed from a chronic physical handicap.

Whichever category your problem falls into, it is difficult when you feel like your prayers aren't being answered, isn't it? Perhaps my experience can help you. I have learned a powerful lesson about how waiting upon the Lord eases our burdens. Waiting upon the Lord implies that you have a firm expectation that the Lord will bless you.

But built into this hope is also a willingness to submit to the Lord's timetable and to His way.

Fifteen years ago my husband, Rick, and I noticed that our third child, Nathan, wasn't developing the same way our other children had. His language was delayed, he had extreme outbursts of temper, and he engaged in repetitive hand-clenching movements. We decided to have a specialist evaluate him. After hours of testing Nate, the doctor asked Rick and me to meet with him privately.

The news we received was devastating. Nate was diagnosed with significant developmental delays and autistic tendencies. His future looked bleak. We were told that Nate would never live a normal life. Among other things, he might need help doing even a simple minimum-wage job and might never be able to live independently.

Our emotions were drained as we returned home to our young family that night. It was all we could do to fix dinner and put the children to bed. Family prayer was especially difficult. Looking across the circle of kneeling children at Nathan was almost more than we could bear. How could this beautiful, blond, curly-haired child be consigned to such a life?

Late into that night and into the wee hours of the morning, I was still unable to sleep. For hours I had been pondering the words of the doctor. I climbed out of bed and went to the living room to once again pour out my heart to Heavenly Father. I wanted a miracle, and I pled with him to heal Nate. I knew that he had the power. I felt that I had the faith. Surely Heavenly Father would heal my son and rescue him from this long, difficult, mortal task. I prayed and sobbed and pounded my fist until my body could no longer bear it. I finally nodded off to sleep in the early hours of dawn.

When I awoke the next day, Nate was playing outside our bedroom door. He was still making repetitive motions and clenching his fists. His temper was raw, and there were outbursts of screaming and crying. His words were few. He was not healed.

Could Heavenly Father have healed Nathan that night? Yes. Sometimes those wonderful miracles do occur, but this time it didn't. And it wasn't because he didn't love Nathan enough or because I didn't have enough faith. Our mortal lives are full of challenges that won't be resolved immediately. That is part of the test. We must learn to conform our wills to Heavenly Father's, just as the Savior did in Gethsemane when he said, "O my Father, if it be possible, let this cup pass from me: nevertheless not as I will, but as thou wilt" (Matthew 26:39).

Now let's look at those problems in that first category, things that can be resolved through the use of someone's agency. Can Heavenly Father force your parents not to get a divorce? No. It would violate their moral agency. He is there to assist them and lead them along, but the choice is still theirs. Can he force a group of kids to accept you? No. His Spirit is there to love and guide them as they come unto Him, but the choice is theirs. That's how agency works. You can and should pray for His Spirit to bless others, but please realize that even Heavenly Father won't override agency. President Spencer W. Kimball said, "Faith must be tested. Some become bitter when oft-repeated prayers seem unanswered. . . . But if all the sick were healed, if all the righteous were protected and the wicked destroyed, the whole program of the Father would be annulled and the basic principle of the gospel, free agency, would be ended" (Edward L. Kimball, ed., *The Teachings of Spencer W. Kimball* [Salt Lake City: Bookcraft, 1982], p. 77).

So does that mean that we must be miserable as we are faced with seemingly unresolvable problems? No! That's where waiting upon the Lord comes in. Perhaps one key lies in being tutored by the Spirit about what to pray for. Let's get back to the Nathan example.

Fifteen years passed after that fist-pounding prayer, and I found myself at Nate's bedside in the intensive care unit at LDS Hospital in Salt Lake City. Nathan's life hung in the balance. He had been hit by a car and had suffered severe brain damage. He was in a coma. The prognosis was bleak. Even if he lived, his life would be dramatically impacted. He may have had to be fed through a feeding tube and may have required twenty-four-hour-a-day nursing care for the rest of his life. He could have been paralyzed. He could have remained in a coma indefinitely. His life and our lives were turned upside down.

Once again I found myself in fervent prayer to my Heavenly Father about my son Nate. But this prayer was completely different than the prayer uttered fifteen years before. Year after year the Lord had led me along through Nate's disabilities. I had felt His loving, gracious Spirit lift and sustain me thousands of times. I had come to know the Lord, and my love and trust in Him had deepened through the years. And so this time my prayer didn't consist of counseling the Lord (see Jacob 4:10). There was neither fist pounding nor demands that this trial be immediately solved according to my blueprint. I was content to wait upon the Lord. And so my prayer went something like this: "Heavenly Father, please bless my dear son. And as for me, show me where you want me to put my feet, and I'll walk that path."

While praying at my son's bedside, did I desire any less for him to have a wonderful life than I had fifteen years before? No. But my waiting upon the Lord for years had broadened my view of this mortal test. The words of Elder Robert D. Hales of the Quorum of the Twelve Apostles explain it best. He said, "My dear brothers and sisters, when pain, tests, and trials come in life, draw near to the Savior. 'Wait upon the Lord, . . . look for him' (Isaiah 8:17; 2 Nephi 18:17). 'They that wait upon the Lord shall renew their strength; they shall mount up with wings as eagles; they shall run, and not be weary; and they shall walk, and not faint' (Isaiah 40:31). Healing comes in the Lord's time and the Lord's way; be patient" ("Think to Thank," *Ensign*, November 1998, p. 17).

I testify with all my heart that Elder Hales's counsel is true. Draw near to the Lord and trust him. He will renew your strength. You can bear any burden with his grace carrying you along. (See under "grace" in the Bible Dictionary.) And eventually the Lord's time and the Lord's way will become your way also.

The strength that the Lord promises takes many forms. As we come unto Christ, He changes us. He makes us stronger. It's kind of like growing up spiritually. I like the way Elder Orson F. Whitney of the Quorum of the Twelve Apostles put it when he said, "All that we suffer and all that we endure, especially when we endure it patiently, builds up our characters, purifies our hearts, expands our souls, and makes us more tender and charitable, more worthy to be called the children of God . . . and it is through sorrow and suffering, toil and tribulation, that we gain the education that we come here to acquire and which will make us more like our Father and Mother in heaven" (quoted in Spencer W. Kimball, *Faith Precedes the Miracle* [Salt Lake

City: Deseret Book Co., 1972], p. 98). Whichever category your problem falls into, the Lord will bless you with these wonderful gifts as you come unto him.

Another way the Lord strengthens us is through the goodness of others. Family, friends, and Church leaders will bless your life through their service. You will come to understand that as these people serve you they are literally on an "errand from the Lord" (Jacob 1:17).

About a year after Nate's accident he recovered enough from his head injury so that he could safely walk around our immediate neighborhood by himself. It had become a favorite nightly ritual for him to leave our home after dinner and visit with a few of our neighbors. We had lived in the same area of Salt Lake for twenty years, and we had a large support group of family and friends that opened their hearts and homes to Nate. But we had no idea how many people were serving our son until his nineteenth birthday arrived.

In the past, Nate had celebrated his birthday with our large extended family. But this year most of the family members were out of town, so we thought it might be nice to invite those neighbors who had been spending time with Nate since the accident. We estimated the circle of friends to include about fifteen families. After presenting the idea to Nate, I asked him to ride around the neighborhood with me. His job was to point out the households that he had been visiting for the past few months. Armed with a legal pad and pencil, we began driving down the street together.

"Mom, stop here. Paula Miller lets me make pies with her. Let's invite her family. Write them on your paper." We stopped the car, and I wrote the Millers' name down. "Stop here, Mom. Brother Mauss had me come by on his birthday to eat cake with his family." We stopped the car and added that family to the list. "Stop here, Mom. Put the Spiers family down on your paper too. Brother Spiers watches *Star Wars* movies with me. I want them to come. Mom, stop again. Write down the Walters' name. They have a flower in their yard that they say is mine. They remind me to come by often to visit them and water it. If I don't come by a lot, the flower might die." We drove a bit further, and Nate said, "Stop here, Mom. Sister Butcher watches a movie with me every Friday. Stop here, Mom. Mr. Barney lets me cut his grass sometimes. I love that! Stop here, Mom. Mrs. Roth used to be my teacher, and she's still my friend. Stop here, Mom. . . Stop here, Mom. . . Stop here, Mom . . ." By the time we were finished, there were over fifty families on our list. Tears streamed down my cheeks as the magnitude of service being offered to Nate became apparent.

The day of the party I went to Costco and filled the family Grand Cherokee with cakes and other treats for the party. When I got home my daughter Jen said, "Mom, it looks like you bought every cake at Costco. What if nobody comes?" I replied, "Jen, we've dealt with autism, head injury, and coma. We can survive unpopularity!"

That night, ten minutes before the party was supposed to begin, the doorbell rang. It was Brother Dave Neeley. He was the stake athletic director and had stopped by early before a night of overseeing volleyball games in the cultural hall. Moments later the doorbell rang again, then again, and again. Dozens of people flooded into our home to honor our Nate the Great.

Throughout the evening I hardly had a chance to break away from my job refilling the buffet table. As I was occupied with that task, I became a bit anxious. Often when Nathan would talk to someone, I would try to be nearby to offer assistance, especially since his head injury. Nate would often click his fingers while rattling off speech at an amazing speed. He would also talk nonstop about the same subject, repeating himself over and over again until the listener was exhausted. In such cases, I'd usually jump in and steer Nate's conversation another direction or clarify to the listener what he was trying to say. It's kind of like being an interpreter for his peculiar form of language. But that evening I was hosting over a hundred people. Being at his side was impossible. All I could do was serve food at the dining room table while Nate worked the crowd alone.

I will never forget what I saw next. Every person that approached Nate knew how to interact with him. They were undaunted by his finger snapping and rambling thoughts. Arms reached around his shoulders and embraced him with love. Stories were shared. Smiles and laughter were exchanged. Everyone was comfortable. And then this wonderful thought occurred to me:

Everyone here "speaks Nathan." They all understood him. And they loved him. But how did they all know what to do? The answer was simple. In the past each of them in their own way had served Nate, and in that service the Spirit had taught them how to interact with him.

As I watched this scene unfold before my eyes, our house became holy ground. In each neighbor's behavior there was a softness and sweetness that was truly Christlike. And I came to see a visual example of the following scripture passage: "And as Jesus passed by, he saw a man which was blind from his birth. And his disciples asked him, saying, Master, who did sin, this man, or his parents, that he was born blind? Jesus answered, Neither hath this man sinned, nor his parents: but that the works of God should be made manifest in him" (John 9:1–3).

Was this scene in our home anything less than the work of God being made manifest? This loving sight was the gospel of Jesus Christ in action. It became apparent that as people had loved and served Nathan they had come to feel the Savior's love also. This evening was only one small example of the impact his life had on those around him. For nineteen years Nate had struggled with his handicap. It had been hard for our family also. But I am so grateful that my fist-pounding prayer of fifteen years ago was answered in the Lord's way and not mine. The difficult handicap that I had been so anxious to pray away had become a marvelous blessing for Nate, our family, and countless others.

I testify that the Lord knows each of us by name and that He is aware of our challenges. And if we come unto Him, we will not be disappointed, for ultimately all that our Father hath can be ours (see D&C 84:38). Perhaps our life's script won't be written exactly as we would have originally desired. But if we let the Lord do the rewrite, the blessings will be indescribable.

"For since the beginning of the world men have not heard, nor perceived by the ear, neither hath the eye seen, O God, beside thee, what he hath prepared for him that waiteth for him" (Isaiah 64:4).

Sue Egan is a homemaker and the mother of six children. She has worked for BYU Youth and Family Programs for nine years. Sue is an avid student of the scriptures and is currently teaching the Gospel Doctrine class in her ward. She and her husband, Rick, reside with their family in Salt Lake City, Utah.

Experiencing a Mighty Change of Heart

Have you ever had a dragon day? Maybe it was a day when your temperament so closely resembled that of a fire-breathing dragon that everyone avoided you for fear of having their heads bitten off. I've had a few days like that before. That is not the only kind of dragon day, however, because there are so many different kinds of dragons: gossiping, pride, fighting with family members, missing church meetings because we don't feel like going, cheating in school, viewing pornography on the Internet—even immorality, road rage, or gang violence. I call days when we fall into one of Satan's temptation traps dragon days because we lose a portion of the Holy Ghost and our natures become more dragon-like than Christlike.

King Benjamin referred to this dragon-like nature as the natural man. He said, "The natural man is an enemy to God." I know none of us ever wants to be an enemy to God. We feel terrible when we fall to temptation and allow that dragon-like nature to come out. Fortunately, King Benjamin also testified that we can put off the natural man "through the atonement of Christ the Lord" (see Mosiah 3:19). I want to bear my testimony along with King Benjamin's: I know that by the power of the Atonement we can overcome this dragon-like natural man! In order to illustrate *how* to do this, I would like to share one of my favorite stories with you from the *Chronicles of Narnia* by C. S. Lewis.

The Parable of the Dragon

Eustace and a group of his friends were taking a sea voyage to the edge of the world. From the very start, Eustace had made life miserable for everyone. He was a chronic complainer, very self-righteous, and selfish, and he refused to do anything for anyone besides himself. In fact, he was about as hard to get along with as anyone you could ever meet. Along their way these voyagers stopped at an island, and as everyone helped unpack the ship and set up camp, Eustace wandered off alone and got lost. Several hours later he stumbled across a cave, and lying lifeless at its opening was an old dragon. At first, Eustace was afraid to go past the dragon and into the cave, but when he did he discovered that the cave was full of treasure! Unable to bear the thought of sharing his newfound treasure with his friends, he stayed up late into the night trying to figure out how to get it off the island without anyone knowing. Finally sleep overtook him, and when he awoke he had—much to his surprise and dismay—become a dragon himself!

Now, I believe the only real difference between Eustace and the rest of us is that on his dragon day his dragon-like nature *got all the way out*. Shocked by his grotesque appearance, he did what anyone would have done: he began to cry. For the first time since they had arrived at the island, he wished he was back with his friends. Running up the hillside to search for them, he suddenly felt his feet lift off the ground as his wings carried him into the air! Off in the distance he could see his friends, and he could hear them calling, "Eustace! Eustace!" When he swooped down to answer their cries, his awful appearance scared them so much they ran into the bushes to hide. Finally, however, they crept out in curiosity because it looked as if the dragon were scratching words in the sand with its claws. As they got close enough, they could see that it said, "It's me—Eustace."

As a fire-breathing dragon, Eustace could have really made their lives miserable. But he was so miserable being a dragon himself he couldn't think of causing problems for anyone else. He had difficulty communicating, his food tasted smokey, he was bulky and uncoordinated, and he was so dreadful-looking he scared even himself. For days he did nothing but mope around feeling sorry for himself. Finally he began to realize that he had done this to himself. What's more, he had made everyone else miserable too. He felt so bad that he wanted to do something to make up for it. After several clumsy attempts to help out, he gave up. The only thing he could do was to light the campfire with his torch-like dragon breath, but everyone had to run for cover to avoid being burnt by the wild flames.

Soon it was time to leave the island. Eustace knew he would have to stay behind; he was just too big to fit aboard the ship. It seemed he was destined to be trapped in the dragon's body and live alone on the island forever.

As he lay quietly sobbing outside camp the night before his companions left, he suddenly felt the presence of something—or someone—behind him. He turned around to see the largest, most magnificent lion you could possibly imagine. (In this story the lion's name is Aslan, and he symbolically represents the King of Kings, Jesus Christ.) Even though he was a dragon, Eustace found himself cowering before the lion's majestic presence. In a deep, commanding voice, the lion simply said, "Come, follow me."

Quietly he followed the lion to the top of the highest peak on the mountainous island. There, in a grove of trees, Eustace saw a beautiful pool of crystal-clear water with emerald-colored steps carved into the side that led down into it. The water looked so clean and refreshing that Eustace wanted to bathe himself in it. But as he was about to enter the water, the lion said, "You must disrobe before you can enter here." At first Eustace was not sure how a dragon could disrobe, but remembering that he was reptile-like, he scratched away at his outer layer of skin, and to his surprise it came off like a banana peel. As he started for the pool the second time, he noticed a second skin below the first. He removed this one the same way, but this time he had to scratch deeper, which caused him intense pain. Much to his dismay, there was another skin below that one. A third time he scratched and clawed, this time drawing blood at every stroke. Finally he removed that skin also, only to see another one below it. Helplessly, he looked towards the lion, who said, "If you will let me, I will help you."

Even though the powerful lion could have easily destroyed him, Eustace lay down and quietly submitted himself to the lion, whose huge claws were much larger and sharper than his own. With one powerful swipe, the lion cut through the outer layers of skin and deep into the flesh of the dragon, causing pain so intense that Eustace thought he was going to die. The lion reached far into the old dragon's body, pulled out Eustace, and cast him through the air into the glimmering pool. The water stung his tender skin at first, but after a moment he emerged whole, clean, and new. Now that he was a young man again, he longed to continue the voyage with his friends. The lion helped Eustace into a new change of clothing he had prepared for him, and then he vanished. Eustace was able to continue on the voyage, this time a happy, content, and helpful companion.

There are three principles concerning the process of putting off the natural man that I would like to draw from this analogy. First, no one can do this without the help of the Savior. Second, pain—also called "godly sorrow" (2 Corinthians 7:10)—is a necessary part of the repentance process. Third, the Lord can change our hearts and natures only if we will come to Him in courage and faith.

We All Need the Savior's Help

In this story Eustace represents all of us as we try to put off the natural man. The dragon's claws were sharp, and our efforts to overcome sin on our own may be noble, but neither is enough. No one can completely put off the natural man by his own efforts. President Ezra Taft Benson explained why this is so: "Repentance means more than simply a reformation of behavior. Many men and women in the world demonstrate great will-power and self-discipline in overcoming bad habits and the weaknesses of the flesh. Yet at the same time they give no thought to the Master, sometimes even openly rejecting Him. Such changes of behavior, even if in a positive direction, do not constitute true repentance. . . . True repentance is based on and flows from faith in the Lord Jesus Christ. There is no other way. *True repentance involves a change of heart and not just a change of behavior*" (*The Teachings of President Ezra Taft Benson* [Salt Lake City: Bookcraft, 1988], p. 71; emphasis added).

While we may shed some sinful behaviors, only the Lord can change our natures, our very beings, so that we experience a mighty change of heart (see Alma 5:14) and become "new creatures" (Mosiah 27:26). Elder Vaughn J. Featherstone of the Seventy related the following story about a young missionary candidate who learned this lesson through his own experience:

> As I invited the young man into my office, . . . I said to him: "Apparently there has been a major transgression in your life. . . . Would you mind being very frank and open and telling me what that transgression was?"
>
> With head held high and in a haughty manner he responded, "There isn't *anything* I haven't done."
>
> I responded: "Well, then, let's be more specific. Have you been involved in fornication?"
>
> Very sarcastically, he said, "I told you I've done *everything*." . . .
>
> I said, "I would to God your transgression was not so serious."
>
> "Well, it is," he replied.
>
> "How about drugs?"
>
> "I told you. I've done *everything*."
>
> Then I said, "What makes you think you're going on a mission?"
>
> "Because I have repented," he replied. "I haven't done any of these things for a year." . . .
>
> I looked at the young man sitting across the desk: twenty-one years old, laughing, sarcastic, haughty, with an attitude far removed from sincere repentance. And I said to him: . . . "You haven't repented; you've just stopped doing something. Someday, after you have been to Gethsemane and back, you'll understand what true repentance is. . . . After you've been to Gethsemane," I continued, "you'll understand what I mean. . . ."
>
> The young man left the office, and I'm sure he wasn't very pleased; I had stood in his way and kept him from going on a mission.
>
> About six months later, I was down in Arizona speaking at the institute. . . . As I looked up I saw this young man—the nonrepentant transgressor—coming down the aisle toward me. . . .
>
> I reached down to shake hands with him, and as he looked up at me I could see that something wonderful had taken place in his life. Tears streamed down his cheeks. An almost holy glow came from his countenance. I said to him, "You've been there, haven't you?"

And through tears he said, "Yes, . . . I've been to Gethsemane and back."

"I know," I said. "It shows in your face. I believe now that the Lord has forgiven you."

He responded: "I'm more grateful to you than you'll ever know for not letting me go on a mission. . . . Thanks for helping me." (*A Generation of Excellence* [Salt Lake City: Bookcraft, 1975], pp. 156–59)

With the help of the Lord, the promise made through the Old Testament prophet Ezekiel can be ours as well: "A new heart also will I give you, and a new spirit will I put within you: and I will take away the stony heart out of your flesh, and I will give you an heart of flesh" (Ezekiel 36:26).

Pain and Sorrow Are Part of the Repentance Process

When Eustace underwent the change from a dragon to a new young man, he experienced so much pain he thought he would die. Killing the dragon-like natural man is painful, but the joy of true repentance is just as real and great as the pain. Remember Alma the Younger's experience? He described it this way: "Yea, I say unto you, my son, that there could be nothing so exquisite and so bitter as were my pains. Yea, and again I say unto you, my son, that on the other hand, there can be nothing so exquisite and sweet as was my joy" (Alma 36:21).

The pain he experienced as he changed from his "carnal and fallen state, to a state of righteousness" (Mosiah 27:25) is a necessary part of the repentance process for everyone. President Spencer W. Kimball taught: "Do you remember what was said by the prophet Alma? 'Now,' he said, 'repentance could not come unto men except there were a punishment.' (Al. 42:16). Ponder on that for a moment. Have you realized that? There can be no forgiveness without real and total repentance, and there can be no repentance without punishment" ("To Bear the Priesthood Worthily," *Ensign,* May 1975, p. 78).

What is that punishment? Alma said, "There was a punishment affixed, . . . which brought remorse of conscience unto man" (Alma 42:18). This remorse of conscience is not the pain that comes from the realization that we have disappointed or hurt others by our actions. Nor is it the embarrassment we experience when our weaknesses become exposed. Although those types of pain are very real, they do not constitute the godly sorrow spoken of by Paul: "Godly sorrow worketh repentance to salvation . . . but the sorrow of the world worketh death" (2 Corinthians 7:10).

What is godly sorrow then? President Benson explained: "Part of this mighty change of heart is to feel godly sorrow for our sins. . . . It is not uncommon to find men and women in the world who feel remorse for the things they do wrong. Sometimes this is because their actions cause them or loved ones great sorrow and misery. Sometimes their sorrow is caused because they are caught and punished for their actions. *Such worldly feelings do not constitute 'godly sorrow.'* Godly sorrow is a gift of the Spirit. It is a deep realization that our actions have offended our Father and our God. It is the sharp and keen awareness that our behavior caused the Savior, . . . the greatest of all, to endure agony and suffering. Our sins caused Him to bleed at every pore. This very real mental and spiritual anguish is what the scriptures refer to as having 'a broken heart and a contrite spirit' (D&C 20:37). Such a spirit is the absolute prerequisite for true repentance" (*The Teachings of President Ezra Taft Benson,* pp. 71–72; emphasis added).

I learned how essential godly sorrow is in the repentance process from an experience I had with one of my former students. She came to me one day with a troubling question. Without sharing the details of her sin with me because true confession is confidential and should be made only to one's bishop, she asked: "How do I feel godly sorrow? I don't even feel bad for what I've done. I know I'm supposed to, but I don't, so I'm afraid I might fall to temptation again. What should I do?" We talked about how godly sorrow is a gift of the Spirit. Because sin separates us from the Holy Ghost, it is possible to sin to the point that we become "past feeling" (1 Nephi 17:45). This young sister resolved to try to get the Spirit back in her life. She went to her bishop and submitted herself to the complete repentance process. She combined her repentance with prayer, scripture study, and faithful obedience over an extended period of time.

When the Spirit finally returned, she had a powerful manifestation of the godly sorrow spoken of in the scriptures. After her experience she reported: "I felt it! I have experienced godly sorrow!" She was sure excited for someone who had gone through so much. She continued: "Once the Spirit came back, I became aware of the seriousness of my sins and how deeply disappointed and sad my Heavenly Father and Jesus were because of me. I realized that the Savior had suffered in the Garden of Gethsemane for *my* sins. I've never felt such intense pain in my heart. It was like being completely engulfed. I cried for hours. But afterwards the peace came, and I realized that the Savior loves me, cares about me, and has done all of this so I could be clean and forgiven. I love him so much for what he has done for me!"

We Need to Have Courage and Faith

It took great courage for Eustace to submit to the lion's hand. It will take courage for us too. But the Lord said: "Be strong and of a good courage; be not afraid, neither be thou dismayed: for the Lord thy God is with thee" (Joshua 1:9). The Lord will be with us too, especially in the process of putting off the natural man. As we try to slay our dragons, if we can have the courage and faith required to submit ourselves to the power of the Savior's love and Atonement, His healing touch can transform us in a wonderful and miraculous way.

King Benjamin's people provide a wonderful example of this. Upon hearing the prophecies concerning the suffering of the Savior for the wickedness of mankind, these people were so overcome they fell "to the earth, for the fear of the Lord had come upon them. And they had viewed themselves in their own carnal [sinful] state, even less than the dust of the earth. And they all cried aloud with one voice, saying: O have mercy, and apply the atoning blood of Christ that we may receive forgiveness of our sins, and our hearts may be purified; for we believe in Jesus Christ" (Mosiah 4:1–2).

Even though they were fearful because of their sins, they had the courage and faith to plead for mercy. Subsequently, they received a mighty change of heart, "and they all cried with one voice, saying: Yea, we believe all the words which thou hast spoken unto us; and also, we know of their surety and truth, because of the Spirit of the Lord Omnipotent, which has wrought a mighty change in us, or in our hearts, that we have no more disposition to do evil, but to do good continually" (Mosiah 5:2).

If we can have the faith and courage to come unto Christ, we too can overcome the natural man and by His miraculous power become completely whole, clean, and new again. President Benson proclaimed: "The miracle of forgiveness is real, and true repentance is accepted of the Lord. . . . We must take our sins to the Lord in humble and sorrowful repentance. We must plead with Him for power to overcome them. The promises are sure. He will come to our aid. We will find the power to change our lives" (*The Teachings of Ezra Taft Benson*, pp. 70, 72).

I know these principles are true. You can trust Him who is your Savior, Redeemer, and friend. I humbly pray that we will all "come unto Christ, who is the Holy One of Israel, and partake of his salvation, and the power of his redemption. Yea, come unto him, and offer your whole souls as an offering unto him, . . . and as the Lord liveth ye will be saved" (Omni 1:26).

Ron Bartholomew was born and raised in Lehi, Utah. After serving a mission in Pusan, Korea, he met his wife, Kristen, while they were both working at the MTC. They are the parents of five children. He attended BYU, where he received a B.A. in Korean language and a master's degree in international relations. He serves as the stake Young Men president and has taught seminary for the past fif-  *teen years. He loves running, bicycling, woodworking, gardening, computers, and especially gummi bears*

"I Think I Can" and Other Brave Thoughts

There was this little train. Actually, he was an engine. As he approached a steep incline he thought, "There is no way I can make it up this mountain." Then he had another thought: *Maybe I need to change my attitude. Instead of thinking I* can't *do this, perhaps I should think about how I* can *do it.* So the little engine repeated to himself, "I think I can; I think I can; I think I can." Slowly he crept up the mountain. With his focus on making it to the top, he paid less attention to the difficulty of making the ascent. With a lot of effort and a lot of "I think I can" thoughts, the brave little engine made it to the top. That is how he came to be known as the little engine that could.

My parents told or read that story to me lots of times when I was small. But it wasn't until I got bigger and older that I had a more clear understanding of the significance of that little engine. He had stamina. He had a good attitude. He had conviction. He had courage. Now, as I navigate life's mountains and valleys, I try to keep a picture of that little stalwart engine clearly in my mind, because life can be difficult and full of challenges. But doesn't it feel great when we hang in there, hold on, and make it through the heartbreak of the hour or up that mountain of the moment?

I want to share with you a few brave thoughts about hanging in there and holding on, about finding the courage and strength to do what is right, about conquering the mountains that loom ahead and rejoicing at overcoming the obstacles that lie in our path. These are things that I need to continually work on as I chug along the track that leads home. I am hoping they might be of help to you too.

The Courage to Make a Difference

If life ever feels a little overwhelming, like it does for me on occasion, these are the times to decide that you won't let problems keep you down. We have to be careful not to wallow in a pity party: you know, that special party at which you are the only guest and everything is terrible and depressing and awful. If the way we react to life's challenges can make or break us, I hope we may react like my friend Jason. Jason was an athletic young man with a promising future in baseball. On a trip to Lake Powell he dove into the water, hit his head on a boulder, and became a quadriplegic. The entire story of his fight to survive and live a useful life is beautiful and inspiring. But it is especially interesting that Jason's practical, day-to-day method of making a difference in his own life is to get rid of the pity party. He says that he limits the whining time to thirty minutes. When the half-hour is up, so is the complaining. It has made a big difference for the better in his life. Because of his courage and determination, he has made a difference in a lot of other lives also! The following poem perfectly sums up Jason's philosophy:

> The Oyster
> There once was an oyster
> Whose story I tell,
> Who found that some sand
> Had got into his shell.
> It was only a grain,
> But it gave him great pain
> For oysters have feelings
> Although they're so plain.
>
> Now, did he berate
> The harsh workings of fate
> That had brought him
> To such a deplorable state?

Did he curse at the government,
Cry for election,
And claim that the sea should
Have given him protection?

No—he said to himself
As he lay on a shell,
Since I cannot remove it
I shall try to improve it.
Now the years have rolled around,
As the years always do,
And he came to his ultimate
Destiny: stew.

And the small grain of sand
That had bothered him so
Was a beautiful pearl
All richly aglow.
Now the tale has a moral,
For isn't it grand
What an oyster can do
With a morsel of sand?

What couldn't we do
If we'd only begin
With some of the things
That get under our skin.

(Anonymous)

Elder Boyd K. Packer of the Quorum of the Twelve Apostles said, "Things we cannot solve, we must survive" ("Balm of Gilead," *Ensign*, November 1987, p. 18). When the going gets tough—and it *will* from time to time—we can pick ourselves up and decide not only to get through it but to get through it well. The very act of getting honorably through the difficulties strengthens our testimony, builds our courage, and keeps us pushing up the mountain.

The Courage to Say No

Joseph is a priesthood leader I am anxious to one day meet. Here is a guy who happens to have a lot going for him. He has the good fortune of being highly favored by his father. His dad even gives him a beautiful coat made of many colors. This doesn't go over too well with his brothers. For being favored, he has the bad fortune of being dumped in a hole and sold as a slave by his brothers. He has the good fortune of being rescued—well, kind of: read Genesis 37 to get the rest of the story—and ends up in the king's court. He has the bad fortune of being good-looking (stay with me: yes, it seems it *can* be a problem sometimes). Potiphar's wife thinks to herself, *This is one good-looking guy* (or something like that) and sets out to seduce him. He has the good sense to say no (see Genesis 39).

Let's stop here for a moment. Joseph was a human being. He surely had feelings and desires and thoughts like other human beings. Potiphar's wife was a powerful woman. Who would know if he gave in to her advances? But Joseph had the courage to say no. He was falsely accused and had the bad fortune of being sent to prison. As we continue reading Genesis 39 we find he has the good fortune of being blessed with the ability to interpret dreams. And because of this ability he comes full circle: back to the king's court and able to save himself and even his brothers who, so many years ago, deserted him. One of the powerful elements in this story is the continual good fortune and bad fortune Joseph encounters throughout his life. He used them all to his good because he had courage. What an example Joseph is!

Let's look at a modern-day example of the courage to say no. Scott was the only member of the LDS Church in his high school. He took a lot of teasing and dealt daily with classmates who dared him to join their weekly drinking parties. There was a big event coming up on Friday night. Everyone wanted Scott to climb down off his pedestal and "be a man," or in other words become a beer drinker. What would it matter if he bent the rules just once? Who would care if he broke the Word of Wisdom just this one time? Friday was a tense day for Scott as he tried to rationalize his decision to attend the party. He lied to his parents about where he was going and headed off to try new things. The party was pretty crazy. Scott was afraid to do something that he knew was wrong, but he was more afraid of looking bad in front of his friends. Someone passed him a drink. All eyes were on him. With his heart pounding, he raised the cup to his mouth. And then he remembered something he had heard President Howard W. Hunter say: "Courage is acting in spite of fear" (in Conference Report, April 1967, p. 117). Scott slowly set down the cup and walked out of the party. He had found the courage to say no.

I wish I could tell you that Scott's high school days were great and everyone applauded him for his decision to act on what he knew was right. The truth is, he was the laughingstock of the junior class. Very few ventured to become his friend. But Scott remained true and faithful. He served a mission and married in the temple. But that isn't the neatest part of the story.

Scott has a younger brother. Jared never had the strength of conviction that seemed to come naturally to Scott. He thought his big brother was a nerd and a loser. But he quietly watched his older brother. More times than Scott would ever know, his good example paved the way for a little brother who remembered the courage of his older sibling. Jared was present at a youth conference where I was teaching. He credited his brother's strength in saying no to improper things for keeping him from going way off track. Tears came to my eyes as I listened to a teenage boy express his love and admiration for the courage of his older brother.

"Sister Pahnke," Jared said, "my brother taught me a scripture that goes, 'Be strong and of a good courage' [Deuteronomy 31:6]. But he didn't just teach me with words; he taught me by his own example."

I thought of another older brother—our Savior—and the perfect example of courage He has provided for us. Have the courage to say no to the things of this world, my friends. The mountains will be easier to climb if you do!

The Courage to Say Yes

We read these powerful words in Deuteronomy 20:1: "When thou goest out to battle against thine enemies, . . . be not afraid of them: for the Lord thy God is with thee." Moses was a man who knew more than a little about courage, wouldn't you say? Think quickly over his life: being placed in a basket and sent down a canal as an infant to escape certain death; being raised by Pharoah's daughter as royalty yet forsaking it for his higher calling; being outcast; dealing with huge numbers of Israelites who weren't willing to follow the Lord's commandments, even after they had been led out of Egypt; facing Pharoah full of faith to show the Lord's power. Moses was a man who understood going into battle against enemies. Again and again he could have said no when it must have seemed hard to say yes: Yes, I will have faith enough to get the chosen people across the Red Sea; Yes, I will lead this group of people out of bondage even though many of them are ungrateful and disobedient; Yes, I will do the things the Lord commands me. I want to meet Moses one day. I want to ask him questions and shake his hand and maybe give him a hug, if he'll let me! He provides wonderful examples of the courage to say yes.

Whether you need that courage to say yes to a calling, yes to helping out when a family member or friend needs you and it's inconvenient or bothersome, or yes in any situation when it might be easier to say no, you are building steam in that testimony engine of yours to get through the obstacles in this life.

The Courage to Wait

As a young teenager I wrote down a quote I found in an old book: "To wait on God, no time is lost—wait on." There have been a number of times when I have prayed fervently for something and the answer was slow in coming. As I think back it becomes clear to me that I *needed* the wait. Finding and utilizing patience was necessary for the development of my character. And the Lord's time is different—and infinitely better—than our own. The waiting, or enduring, gives us an extra push as we trek up our mountains. President Ezra Taft Benson counseled us, "Daily, constantly, we choose by our desires, our thoughts, and our actions whether we want to be blessed or cursed, happy or miserable. One of the trials of life is that we do not usually receive immediately the full blessing for righteousness or the full cursing for wickedness. That it will come is certain, but oft-times there is a waiting period that occurs. . . . During this testing time the righteous must continue to love God, trust in His promises, be patient, and be assured" ("The Great Commandment—Love the Lord," *Ensign*, May 1988, p. 6).

My young brothers and sisters, we chose to follow the Savior in our premortal state. We honorably and courageously fought for the privilege of coming into this mortal state. If things are difficult for you right now, hold steady and stay on track. If you are experiencing no problems and it is smooth sailing for you, enjoy it. It will most certainly change. The bumps and potholes and obstacles are the very things that help us develop the stamina and attitude and courage to continue on this earthly journey. As we seek first the kingdom of God (see Matthew 6:33), we may be amazed at how we are able to hang in there and hold on.

God bless us to think brave thoughts, adjust our attitudes, and make the required effort to succeed. May He assist us as we muster up the courage to say yes when needed and no when appropriate, to make a difference in our own lives as well as in the lives of those around us, and to wait for the perfect direction of the Father as He directs us along our onward track.

Vickey Pahnke studied musical theater at Brigham Young University after joining the Church as a teenager. She later received a master's degree in communications. She works as a songwriter, producer, and author. Vickey and her husband, Bob, are the parents of four children. She has been involved with many of the BYU youth programs—such as Especially for Youth, Best of Especially for  *Youth, and Outreach Youth conferences—and has been a speaker for the Know Your Religion and BYU Education Week series. She loves mountains, laughter, the ocean, kids of all ages, music, food, and cooking. But mostly, she loves being a mom.*

All Things Testify of Christ

One half mile west of the mouth of Provo Canyon in Utah sits a stone marker. A metal plaque reads simply, "In memory of Travis Chad Robison, 1995." Several joggers, walkers, and bikers see the monument each day adjacent to the pathway that was constructed after the accident. The pathway parallels the roadway filled with vehicles traveling at high rates of speed. Some of the passersby understand why the marker is there, but others do not. The red-sandstone monument has been placed there as a memorial to the courageous young man who gave his life so that his sister could live.

Travis and his sister had been walking east on the edge of that treacherous stretch of highway near the subdivision where they lived. The time of day was almost sunset, which made visibility difficult for motorists traveling in a westerly direction. As the roadway left the canyon, it rose on a steep incline. This often caused drivers to be met with the blinding rays of the setting sun directly in their eyes as they neared the brink of the hill.

Travis and his sister were making their way along the edge of this heavily traveled road as cars, trucks, and vehicles of all shapes and sizes thundered by. Suddenly Travis noticed an oncoming car dangerously close to the road's edge. He immediately realized the danger to both himself and his sister. There was no time for deliberation, discussion, or weighing the outcomes of alternative courses of action. A split-second decision had to be made. Travis made the decision. He selflessly pushed his little sister out of the path of the oncoming car, ensuring her safety but endangering his own. His heroic choice saved her life but ended his. Travis was struck by the car and killed on that fateful day as he courageously sacrificed his own life to preserve the life of someone he loved. Travis was only ten years old.

The years come and go, but the monument remains as a symbol of a young boy's courage, love, and sacrifice. A few people know the story and reverence the monument as a sacred symbol of a brother's devotion to his sister. Others pass the monument, either unaware of its existence or semiconsciously supposing that it must represent something about which they could only guess.

For us during our lives in mortality, the Lord has placed many monuments or symbols in this world. Some are obvious; some are not. It's about understanding these symbols that this chapter was written. Some of those symbols or monuments are listed below. They all share a common theme. Can you discern what that theme is?

Bears hibernating
Trees losing their leaves
    in the fall
New leaves coming forth
    in the spring
Joseph Smith's birthday
Going to bed at night
Grass dying when not watered
The landing of the ark
The spring equinox
A full moon

Jonah and the whale
The Provo Temple
The earth revolving around
    the sun
Manna
The exodus led by Moses
The lives of Abraham,
        Joseph, and Abinadi
Joshua leading Israel across
    the Jordan River
Summer and winter solstice

Each of these events, people, or places all have one common element: they all testify of Christ. How is that possible? The prophet Nephi said, "All things which have been given of God from the beginning of the world, unto man, are the typifying of him [Christ]" (2 Nephi 11:4). Jesus himself revealed to the prophet Enoch the following: "And behold, all things have their likeness, and all things are created and made to bear record of me, both things which are temporal, and things which are spiritual; things which are in the heavens above, and things which are on the earth, and things which are in the earth, and things which are under the earth, both above and beneath: all things bear record of me" (Moses 6:63).

Everything on this earth bears record of Christ! If the scriptures declare this to be true, then why aren't all these things that bear record of Christ more obvious? The answer is simply that the things which testify of Christ are given by the Lord as symbols called types and shadows. A type is a symbol of something that is in the future, and a shadow is a symbol of something that was in the past. For example, in ancient Israel priests holding the Aaronic Priesthood sacrificed male, firstborn, unblemished lambs as a type, or in similitude of, Jesus' sacrifice. Jesus, or the Lamb of God, was also male, the firstborn spirit child of the Father, and sinless. From the reverse perspective, the sacrament is a shadow of Christ's sacrifice. The symbols of the bread and water point back in time and symbolize the sacrifice of Christ's body and blood in Gethsemane and on the cross.

What was one of Jesus' primary methods of teaching? He often used parables. To teach with parables is to teach with symbols. By using parables Jesus would place a spiritual meaning side by side with an everyday event. The parables in Matthew 13 provide us with several examples. In the parable of the sower, the four types of soil represent four categories of people. In the parable of the wheat and the tares, the wheat represents the children of the kingdom and the tares represent the children of the devil. In the parable of the mustard seed, the seed planted in the earth represents the Book of Mormon, and the tree that grew out of the seed represents the church that came forth as a result of the Book of Mormon (see *Teachings of the Prophet Joseph Smith,* comp. Joseph Fielding Smith [Salt Lake City: Deseret Book Co., 1977], pp. 94–99). Let us now explore some examples of types and shadows in three areas: events, people, and things.

Events

The events involved with the coming forth of the Book of Mormon from within the earth closely parallel or symbolize the events involved with Christ's life, death, and resurrection. Robert

Norman, an instructor at the LDS Institute near the University of Utah, discovered the following parallels:

The Book of Mormon—A Typification of Christ
2 Nephi 11:4

Book of Mormon	*Jesus Christ*
A. Coming forth declared by an angel—Moroni	A. Coming forth declared by an angel—Gabriel
B. Come to restore in time of apostasy	B. Came to restore in time of apostasy
C. Laid away in a stone receptacle	C. Laid away in a stone receptacle
D. Taken from receptacle by *Joseph* Smith	D. Put into the receptacle by *Joseph* of Arimathea
E. Came forth after stone was rolled away	E. Came forth after stone was rolled away
F. Angel oversaw coming forth from receptacle	F. Angel oversaw coming forth from receptacle
G. First one to see (Joseph) forbidden to touch	G. First one to see (Mary) forbidden to touch
H. Attested to by twelve witnesses	H. Attested to by twelve witnesses
I. The Word of God	I. The Word of God
J. Teaches fulness of the gospel	J. Teaches fulness of the gospel
K. Keystone of our religion	K. Cornerstone of our church

The Bible Dictionary explains that the journey of Israel from Egypt, through the wilderness, and back to the promised land was a symbol of man's journey from this world, through a millennial era, and back to the presence of God (see "Pauline Epistles: Epistle to the Hebrews," item 6b, p. 747). Other parallels we find here are very striking. We now live in a telestial world. To enter a celestial world we need to be baptized and receive the Holy Ghost. We need to follow Christ. The earth will be changed from a telestial world to a terrestrial world at the time of the Second Coming. It will remain terrestrial for one thousand years before it is changed again at the end of the Millennium and becomes the celestial kingdom. The life the Israelites lived in Egypt symbolized a telestial world. Pharaoh, as a symbol of Satan, had the Israelites in bondage. They needed to follow Moses, a symbol of Christ, to get to a better world, the land of Canaan. How was Moses able to free the Israelites from Egyptian bondage? He had the people put the blood of a firstborn, male, unblemished lamb upon their doorposts. How are we released from the bondage of sin in this telestial world? We must symbolically put the atoning blood of Christ on the doorposts of our lives. We do this through faith in the atoning blood of Christ, repentance of our sins, and a movement away from the corruptions of the world.

How did Israel leave Egypt? They went through the Red Sea as a pillar of fire held back the Egyptians. Therefore, they were saved by water and by fire. How are we saved from this world? We also are saved by the water of baptism and by the fire of the Holy Ghost (see John 3:5). Paul told the Corinthians that Israel's passing through the Red Sea was a symbol of these two cleansings (see 1 Corinthians 10:1–4).

The forty years in the wilderness helped purify Israel before they entered the promised land. The one thousand years of the Millennium will purify the earth before it becomes the celestial kingdom. What the wilderness was for Israel the Millennium will be for us. What did Israel eat? They ate manna. What was manna? It was bread from heaven. Who was the Bread of Life? Jesus (see John 6:33). Where did he come from? Heaven. Where was he born? Bethlehem. What does Bethlehem mean? House of bread (see Bible Dictionary, "Bethlehem," p. 621). What did Israel drink? Water. Who is the living water? Jesus (see John 4:10–14). Where did Israel get the water? From a rock (see Exodus 17:6). Who is the rock? Jesus (see Helaman 5:12). All things actually do testify of Christ!

How did the Israelites get into the promised land? They went *through* the Jordan River (see Joshua 3:16–17). Why go through a river? It symbolized being born again. Where Israel crossed the Jordan River was near where Jesus was later baptized (see Bible Dictionary, "Jordan River," p. 716). Why was Jesus baptized there? Because it is the lowest body of fresh water on the earth, and his baptism symbolized Jesus descending below all things (see Russell M. Nelson, "Self-Mastery," *Ensign*, November 1985, p. 32). Who was it that led Israel through the Jordan River? It was Joshua, who was a symbol of Jesus: Joshua is the Hebrew word for the word in Greek that means Jesus. What preceded Israel leaving Egypt? Plagues. What will precede the Second Coming of Christ before we enter into the Millennium? Plagues! The exodus of Israel from Egypt led by Moses through the wilderness to the promised land is a symbol of our journey from this world led by Christ through the Millennium to a celestial world.

People

In the Book of Mormon the prophet Jacob taught Sherem that every true prophet who ever lived always testified of Christ (see Jacob 7:11). Abinadi preached the same doctrine to King Noah's court (see Mosiah 13:33). Not only did all prophets testify of Jesus, but their lives, names, and missions were also types of Christ. Isaiah's name means "the Lord is salvation" (Bible Dictionary, p. 707). Abraham means "father of a multitude" (Bible Dictionary, p. 601). Even the simple name Joseph Smith is a symbol. Joseph in Hebrew means "may God add sons." A smith is someone who forges or fashions something out of raw material. The Lord called a young boy of that name to be a prophet and forged a kingdom or church through him and then added converts to it. Joseph's name was also known to Joseph who was sold into Egypt 3,500 years before Joseph Smith's birth. (see 2 Nephi 3:6-15; Joseph Smith Translation, Genesis 50:26–33).

When was Joseph Smith born? He was born on December 23rd, at the time of the year astronomers call winter solstice. What happens at winter solstice? The days begin to get longer and more light comes into the world. As Joseph Smith was born, *light was coming into the world*. What happened at Jesus' birth? There were three days of light. As Jesus was born more light came into the world. When was Joseph Smith killed? On June 27—near the summer solstice, when the days are getting shorter. At Joseph's death *light was going out of the world*. What happened at the time of Jesus' death? There were three days of darkness. As Jesus was killed, light went out of the world.

The prophet Jacob wrote that Abraham's offering of Isaac was a "similitude of God and his Only Begotten Son" (Jacob 4:5). The original event is recounted in Genesis 22. The events of Abraham's experience closely parallel those of Jesus'. The Lord told Abraham to take his only son, Isaac, to a mountaintop. Likewise, Jesus was God's only begotten son in the flesh. What mountain was it? It was Mount Moriah. Today Jerusalem sits on top of Mount Moriah. Isaac was to be sacrificed in the same place and on the same mountaintop where Jesus would be crucified. Solomon's temple was built upon this same mount. (See Bible Dictionary, "Moriah," p. 734). Aaronic priests sacrificed lambs as symbols of Christ on the *north side* of the temple altar (see Leviticus 1:11). Later Jesus himself was sacrificed on a hilltop called Golgotha that is located just *north* of the temple altar. It is possible Isaac rode a donkey to the mountain (Genesis 22:3) just as Jesus rode a donkey into Jerusalem (Matthew 21:1–10). Isaac carried the wood for the sacrifice up the hill; Jesus carried the cross up the hill. Isaac was not a teenager, as is commonly depicted, but was in his thirties (*Old Testament Student Manual, Genesis–2 Samuel* [Salt Lake City: The Church of Jesus Christ of Latter-day Saints, 1981], p.78); Jesus was thirty-three when he was crucified. Abraham bound Isaac's hands; Christ's hands were bound to the cross. Isaac's blood was to be shed; Jesus shed His blood in Gethsemane (see Luke 22:44). An angel appeared prior to the sacrifice of Isaac; an angel appeared in Gethsemane (see Luke 22:43). Abraham named the place "Jehovah-jireh" (Genesis 22:14), which means, "In a mount the Lord shall be manifest" (footnote 14b).

Joseph who was sold into Egypt was also a type or symbol of Christ. Joseph was a shepherd (see Genesis 37:2), as was Jesus (see John 10:14). His brothers hated him (see Genesis 37:4-5), as did Jesus' brethren (see John 15:18). Both Joseph and Jesus were betrayed by Judah (Judas is the Greek spelling of the name Judah) for the price of a slave (see Genesis 37:26–28; Matthew 27:3). Joseph was put into a pit (see Genesis 37:24); some traditions say that it was for three days. Jesus was in the tomb three days (see Matthew 12:40). Both Jesus and Joseph came forth from their imprisonments to save the lives of their brethren. When Joseph's eleven brothers came to Egypt looking for food, they didn't recognize their brother Joseph (see Genesis 42:6–8, 45:1). When Jesus appeared to the eleven Apostles, they also didn't recognize him (see Luke 24:36–39). Joseph provided food for his brethren (see Genesis 42:25). Jesus provides spiritual food for all of us as the Bread of Life (see John 6:48–57).

Things

The Lord revealed to Moses that he put the "lights in the firmament" to "be for signs" (Genesis 1:14). What kind of signs? Signs that testify of Christ and his plan of salvation. When the Israelites left Egypt, the destroying angel passed over them but slew the firstborn of the Egyptian families. As a result, this time of year became known as Passover and was celebrated with a Feast of the Passover. The date at which Passover is held is determined by the phases of the moon. Since Israel escaped during a full moon, Passover is determined each year by the first full moon after the spring equinox. Each year the spring equinox is March 21, when the days and nights are of equal length. For this reason, Passover is on a different day each year because the day is decided by the changing phase of the moon, one of the "lights in the firmament." Therefore, Passover is celebrated on a day sometime within a month after March 21, since the moon has a twenty-eight-day cycle.

How does all of this relate to Christ? Our sun is a symbol of the Son of God. The sun comes from the east. You can't look upon it with the naked eye. It gives life to all things. It also destroys all living things that don't receive water. Jesus Christ the Son will return from the east. Righteous people will be saved by the light of his coming (see 1 Nephi 22:17), while the wicked who symbolically would not partake of the living water, who is Christ, will be burned at his coming (see 1 Nephi 22:15). In D&C 88:25 the Lord states that the "earth abideth the law of a celestial kingdom." How does it do that? The earth revolves around the sun. If we are to live a celestial law, we too should have our lives revolve around the Son of God and have Him as the central focus of our lives.

A close examination of several important historical events will reveal that they took place at the Passover season. Among other events, the list would include: the time that the flood waters dried up, the sacrifice of Isaac, Israel crossing the Red Sea, Israel crossing the Jordan River, Christ's birth, the Last Supper (at which the Savior introduced the sacrament), the night in Gethsemane, the Crucifixion, the Resurrection, the publishing of the Book of Mormon, the organization of the Church, the return of Elias, Moses, and Elijah to the Kirtland Temple, and the dedication of the Salt Lake Temple. The First Vision was also very possibly at Passover. Why did all of these events occur at Passover? Why is Passover so significant? It was not the Passover but the Atonement that was the focal point. All of these events were either types pointing toward the Atonement or shadows pointing back to the Atonement. Passover is always at a full moon. A full moon reflects the full light of the sun. The Passover reflects the full weight of the Atonement accomplished by the Son of God.

In Moses 6:63 the Lord states, "All things have their likeness, and all things are created and made to bear record of me, . . . things which are on the earth, and things which are in the earth." Have you ever pondered about what the different things in nature are that bear record of Christ? During the fall, trees lose their leaves. They appear dead throughout the winter. Then miraculously each spring around Passover, tiny, green leaves begin to shoot forth from the branches of these seemingly dead trees. The world becomes green and alive again as though awakened from a deep sleep. Is this not a symbol of Christ's death, burial and resurrection? Why do bears hibernate and then come alive in the spring? Is it not a symbol of death and resurrection? Sometimes we are so close to a symbol we don't recognize it. What is the reason for going to bed at night? Just to rest? No. You symbolically die! Have you ever looked at sleeping people? They look dead. Why do you get up each morning? Just to go to school? No! You symbolically resurrect every morning. Have you ever looked at your friends when they first get up in the morning after a sleep over? They look like they've come back from the dead. All things testify of Christ.

When asked by the Pharisees for a sign, Jesus told them they would get no sign except the sign of the prophet Jonah. "For as Jonas was three days and three nights in the whale's belly; so shall the Son of man be three days and three nights in the heart of the earth" (see Matthew 12:39–40). Most of us know the story of Jonah being inside the whale for three days and coming out alive, but how many of us realize the event is a symbol of Christ's being in the tomb for three days and coming out alive?

A monument stands at the mouth of Provo Canyon as a symbol or memorial for Travis Robison. It represents him, his life, his sacrifice, and his death. After we are resurrected, the books will be opened to reveal the record from which we will be judged. It will contain the record of our life, our sacrifices, and our death. It is my prayer that just as the stone marker stands as a monument of Travis's life as one that typified Christ, so may the record of our lives stand as a monument that in every way typifies the life of Jesus Christ.

Holding a bachelor's degree in English, an M.E.D. in counseling and guidance, and and Ed.D. in educational psychology, Todd B. Parker is an associate professor of ancient scripture at Brigham Young University. Dr. Parker was a seminary teacher for fourteen years, and he has also been an institute instructor. An athlete himself, he remains interested in distance running, pole vaulting, gymnastics, and  *in coaching track. He is married to Debra Harbertson, and they have nine children. He currently serves as bishop of the Orem Canyon View Fifth Ward in Orem, Utah.*

Revelation

Several years ago I had the opportunity of teaching in the Church Educational System in the state of Idaho. I taught there for about twenty years, and near the end I started receiving phone calls from administrators asking, "Would you be interested in going to such-and-such a place to teach?" or "Would you like to go to this institute?" or "Would you be interested in being a coordinator?" But I never felt good about those opportunities. On one occasion, however, I was in my office when the phone rang. The individual on the other end of the line offered an opportunity for me to come work in the LDS Church Office Building in Salt Lake City. Instantly I felt an impression that this was what I was supposed to do.

I love teaching, and I love the youth. I didn't want to leave the classroom and be stuck in front of a computer and type all day. They asked if I would work in CES curriculum. I replied that I wanted to go home and talk to my wife and my children to give them an opportunity to be a part of the decision, even though I knew that we were going to go. I wept as I went to the classroom and as I started to teach. The class probably thought, *Boy, Brother Bird is really having a great message today. It's touching only himself.*

As I met with my family, I opened my scriptures and taught them the story of Lehi and how he and his family fled Jerusalem and went into the wilderness. I told my family that we were about to leave and go into the wilderness: Salt Lake City. To me, leaving a small Idaho community and going to a large community was similar to going into a wilderness. One daughter said, "This is a joke isn't it?" Another child said, "Nice try, Dad. What lesson are you trying to teach this time?" But the real answer was that we were going to relocate to a new area, which I am sure many of you have done before.

Isn't it amazing that we sometimes base all of these wonderful decisions that we make on a prompting or a feeling that comes to us from the Holy Ghost? I always marveled at sisters who, when their husbands would say, "We're moving. Time to go," would say, "Oh, this is wonderful. Here we go again," and off they would go to a new area. They are so supportive when we receive inspiration for our family.

Shortly after I came to Utah, I was called to serve as a stake president. I thought, *Maybe this is really the reason I was supposed to be here.* I wasn't sure, but it gave me a bit more of a reason as to why I felt inspired to move.

On one occasion, I was seated in my office issuing a temple recommend to an individual. The person came in and sat down, and I proceeded to ask the temple recommend questions. This person answered all the questions correctly, but I didn't feel good about it. I began to analyze in my own mind whether it was just me. Maybe something wasn't right at work or at home that day, or maybe I was disturbed about dogs running through my new grass and destroying it. I kept wondering, Was it me, or was there something the Lord was trying to teach me about this individual?

I sat there feeling uneasy, and I quickly decided that there were two questions I had to ask this individual. These two questions I asked were not part of the list of questions for the temple recommend, so I asked this person if it would be all right if I asked these additional questions. The person agreed. Similar questions have since been added to our temple recommend book.

The first question was, How do you feel about the Atonement of Jesus Christ? This person answered, "You know, that is a false teaching in this church. No person should have to pay for the sins or transgressions of another." I thought that was interesting. Second question: How do you feel about the Restoration of this Church and gospel? The person said, "You know, the Church is for the weak. It's a social organization to help the weak come together and feel better.

But no, there was no restoration, and no, you don't need a church to perform those things that exalt you."

I looked at this person and said, "Those are interesting answers. This social organization that you just described has just denied you a recommend to enter the house of the Lord." Since that time, we have had the opportunity to teach each other what I thought and what he thought concerning the Atonement and the Restoration of the gospel.

I think it would be wise for all of us to better learn what revelation is and the principles of receiving revelation.

First, revelation is the process that God uses to communicate intelligence, light, and truth to man. The scriptures teach, "Man was also in the beginning with God. Intelligence, or the light of truth, was not created or made, neither indeed can be" (D&C 93:29). Verse 36 says, "The glory of God is intelligence, or, in other words, light and truth." It's important for us to understand that revelation comes in only one way: from God to man. We do not reveal anything to God. I think D&C 38 helps us understand that. In verse two the Lord says he is "the same which knoweth all things, for all things are present before mine eyes." God knows all things. He knows what we need. We are not going to surprise Him with anything in our life.

Second, this light and knowledge is communicated in a Spirit-to-spirit process. I think the Prophet Joseph Smith taught it well when he said, "All things whatsoever God in his infinite wisdom has seen fit and proper to reveal to us, while we are dwelling in mortality, . . . are revealed to us in the abstract, and independent of affinity of this mortal tabernacle, but are revealed to our spirits precisely as though we had no bodies at all; and those revelations which will save our spirits will save our bodies" (*Teachings of the Prophet Joseph Smith,* sel. Joseph Fielding Smith [Salt Lake City: Deseret Book Co., 1977], p. 355). It must be understood that although revelation may involve other senses, such as hearing or sight, without the Spirit's involvement there will be no true revelation.

Third, revelation is the foundation, or rock, that this church is built upon. President Spencer W. Kimball said, "The restored church of Jesus Christ is founded upon the rock of revelation. Continuous revelation is indeed the very lifeblood of the gospel of the living Lord and Savior, Jesus Christ" ("Revelation: The Word of the Lord to His Prophets," *Ensign,* May 1977, p. 76). The Savior said to Peter, "Blessed art thou, Simon Bar-jona: for flesh and blood hath not revealed it unto thee, but my Father which is in heaven. And I say also unto thee, That thou art Peter, and upon this rock I will build my church; and the gates of hell shall not prevail against it" (Matthew 16:17–18).

Fourth, revelation is the only way to know God and His ways. We cannot know God without the Spirit. Paul teaches us, "For what man knoweth the things of a man, save the spirit of man which is in him? even so the things of God knoweth no man, but the Spirit of God" (1 Corinthians 2:11). The Prophet Joseph Smith added, "We never can comprehend the things of God and of heaven, but by revelation" (*Teachings*, p. 292)."

Fifth, there are counterfeit revelations. They can come from Satan or from our own emotions. While I was teaching seminary, young men and young women were always trying to decide if someone was spiritual. If there was a good lesson, they would look around the room and see how many people were crying. The young women would look around and say, "There's one, there's two, there's—we have three spiritual boys in our class." I don't know what the boys were looking for; the girls were always crying.

We have to be careful that we don't get our emotions and the Spirit confused. It's okay if tears accompany the Spirit, but it is not necessary as a sign that the Spirit is present. On one occasion, we had a young man bear his testimony. He had suffered an accident playing basketball. He had gone up for a layup and was undercut by an opposing player. The young man came down on his neck and head. He was rushed to the hospital, and on the way there his father, who was in the ambulance with him, called him back to life through the power of the priesthood. He was able to continue on with his life.

As this young man shared this story with the class, he began to weep. Now, when young women see young men crying, they have this great ability to join in. I guess it's a law that they teach in their Young Women classes around the Church. They started handing out Kleenex. It got to the point that I thought we needed life preservers.

Then I looked at the young men. Some of them were in tears. Now, is that a gauge of spirituality? Maybe. Does it mean that the Spirit is there if the girls have Kleenex? Possibly, but please don't use that as the standard to gauge if the Spirit is present.

President Boyd K. Packer of the Quorum of the Twelve Apostles said, "Be ever on guard lest you be deceived by inspiration from an unworthy source. You can be given false spiritual messages. There are counterfeit spirits just as there are counterfeit angels. . . . The spiritual part of us and the emotional part of us are so closely linked that [it] is possible to mistake an emotional impulse for something spiritual. We occasionally find people who receive what they assume to be spiritual promptings from God, when those promptings are either centered in the emotions or are from the adversary" ("The Candle of the Lord," *Ensign,* January 1983, pp. 55–56).

I have now given you five points to help you understand what revelation is. Let's now go over the principles that govern the giving and receiving of revelation.

First, it is the Lord and not us who determines who will receive revelation, when it is given, how it is given, and what is revealed. As a bishop, I assigned myself to home teach those people in my ward who had gone through Church discipline or who, for some reason or other, were offended and didn't like to attend. I had a large list at the beginning. On one occasion I went to the home of an elderly lady. I had a young Aaronic Priesthood teacher with me. After this lady opened the door, she said, "I don't need you, and I don't need him. Please leave." That was our first response and greeting from this sister. We visited with her on the doorstep for a few minutes and then left. That poor Aaronic Priesthood holder: he thought everybody loved home teachers.

We went a second time and a third time. We went every month. Finally she invited us in. The trailer was rather small. As a matter of fact, it was really small. It was full of garbage, cigarette butts, and beer cans. It was a mess. When we sat down, she said, "I don't want you to give me any great spiritual messages. Let's just visit." Well, we did that for quite some time.

A while later, my wife and I were going to have the opportunity of going to Israel on a tour. I thought it would be nice if I let this dear sister know that we were not going to be at her home this month to home teach. When we arrived at her home, I told her, "I will be gone to Israel for a month, so we won't be here."

She looked at me and said, "You're . . . you're going to Israel? Just a minute." She ran to the back of her trailer and came back with an envelope. She said, "Today is my birthday." I felt bad because maybe she thought I was there to wish her a happy birthday, so I did. Then she said, "My children sent me this money. Will you take it to Israel with you?" She handed me this envelope with one hundred dollars in it.

I told her, "No, I would rather not take your money. Thank you." And then we left. She began calling people within the ward boundaries and having them call me and they would say, "Please come and get her money and take it to Israel." I didn't want that responsibility. But she continued to call often about it.

She finally called my wife. I listen to my wife. She said, "Go get that money." So I went back to her trailer and told her that I really didn't want to take her money.

She said, "It's not for you. You'll know what to do with it when you get to Israel." So I took the money and went to the bank and changed it into one hundred one-dollar bills. They say that's the best way to carry money in Israel. It's easier to exchange one-dollar bills for things that you want to get.

As we toured Israel, I had the distinct impression to get three things with this hundred dollars. First we purchased some books for the BYU Jerusalem Center. The second thing we bought was some trees that would be planted on the Mount of Olives. They gave us certificates that said these trees were donated by this good sister.

From our hotel, if we looked straight down we could see an old pillbox bunker from World War II in which an Arab family lived. We would watch them every day, and we would see the little children sleep on top. So with the rest of this hundred dollars we purchased T-shirts, hats, candy, and gum and put those items, along with what was left of the money, into a box. I then went down to the hotel's main desk and asked, "Would you please write in Arabic that this is a gift from members of The Church of Jesus Christ of Latter-day Saints." I hope that's what they wrote. I wasn't sure because I didn't know Arabic.

My wife and I then went down and gave these parents the gift with the note. The little children had a great time with the chewing gum. They bowed and said thank you in Arabic.

When I returned home, I went to this good sister's trailer. I knocked on the door and said, "I am here to report what we did with your money."

She said, "You don't need to report what you did with my money. I know you did what the Lord wanted you to do."

I told her, "You gave me the money. Now you are going to hear a report on what I did with it." We sat down, and I told her that we bought some books to put in the library. She thought that was nice. I told her what we had done for the small Arab family. She was pleased with that. Then I said, "We bought some trees that were planted on the Mount of Olives."

Her eyes got great big and she said, "How did you know? How did you know that everywhere I live I plant a tree? That's wonderful." I gave her the certificates. She got excited and said, "You know, I wouldn't be surprised if one day the Savior walks among my trees. Now, do you know what He wants me to do with these trees?" I told her that I didn't, and then I asked her what it was he wanted her to do. She said, "He would like me to give them away." So she handed out the certificates in the community, saying, "Here is a tree that you now own on the Mount of Olives." Later she looked at me and said, "I know what you're thinking, young man." I liked the young man part. "I want you to know," and she pointed to her knees, "these knees know God." On fast Sunday this good sister wouldn't give the fast offering to the deacon; she had to personally hand it to me. Often the envelope would contain a rather large contribution. This good sister has since passed away, and I got to speak at her funeral.

The Savior taught us well when he said, "O my Father, if it be possible, let this cup pass from me: nevertheless not as I will, but as thou wilt" (Matthew 26:39). Each of us must submit our will to the Lord on His timetable. Some people on the Lord's timetable receive some remarkable manifestations of the Spirit. Others wanting some of those manifestations wonder why they don't get that kind of an experience in their life. I remember visiting people who had lost a loved one and who said, "It's not fair. I talked to someone who had this great spiritual experience after the death of a loved one. I have not had such a thing." But it's the Lord who knows what's best for each and every one of us.

In Alma 18, some people had remarkable experiences, such as King Lamoni, while others didn't even know what was going on. For example, "And it came to pass that after [Ammon] had said all these things, and expounded them to the king, that the king believed all his words. And he began to cry unto the Lord, saying: "O Lord, have mercy; according to thy abundant mercy which thou hast had upon the people of Nephi, have upon me, and my people. And now, when he had said this, he fell unto the earth, as if he were dead" (vv. 40–42).

King Lamoni had a great experience with the Spirit, but wouldn't it be interesting if you were a missionary and this was the only way people received a testimony? What if every time you bore witness and the Spirit bore witness to them, they fell as if dead? Quite an experience would be written in your journals!

Verse 43 says, "And it came to pass that his servants took him and carried him in unto his wife, and laid him upon a bed; and he lay as if he were dead for the space of two days and two nights; and his wife, and his sons, and his daughters mourned over him, after the manner of the Lamanites, greatly lamenting his loss."

The great prophet Isaiah taught us that it's the Lord who's in control: "For my thoughts are not your thoughts, neither are your ways my ways, saith the Lord. For as the heavens are higher than the earth, so are my ways higher than your ways, and my thoughts than your thoughts" (Isaiah 55:8–9).

Second, most revelation comes through the quiet whisperings of the Spirit. The sensational and dramatic spiritual experiences are real but are the exception rather than the rule. President Packer said, "The Spirit does not get our attention by shouting or shaking us with a heavy hand. Rather it whispers. It caresses so gently that if we are preoccupied we may not feel it at all. . . . Occasionally it will press just firmly enough for us to pay heed. But most of the time, if we do not heed the gentle feeling, the Spirit will withdraw and wait until we come seeking and listening" ("The Candle of the Lord," p. 53). As we communicate with the Lord, it is critical for each of us to clear our minds of the cares of the day, of the problems, struggles, and frustrations. Maybe we could find a closet somewhere to get away from it all, or go for a walk, or whatever else is necessary.

I'm reminded of when auxiliary presidents would come to me when I was a bishop and turn in a list of possible counselors or teachers. Then they would come back the following week and say, "Well, do we have a name for this organization?" However, some weeks were not good for me. Perhaps work and other pressures had been unreal, so I did not have time to receive any clear impressions. In such cases, I just had to tell those good brothers and sisters that I didn't have a name for them yet.

I often wondered what they thought as they walked away. I wondered if they thought, *What kind of a bishop do we have? Can't he even take the time? We fasted and prayed. Why doesn't he get on the ball?* But I didn't want to move forward unless the Lord spoke to me.

We must be careful that we don't covet dramatic experiences or answers to prayers for our testimonies to be built upon. For example, a young lady should never ask, "I want to marry so-and-so. If it is to be, please make his picture float across the room to let me know that he is the one." That would be setting a condition on the Lord and expecting something dramatic to occur.

President Kimball said, "In our day, as in times past, many people expect that if there be revelation it will come with awe-inspiring, earth-shaking display" ("Revelation," p. 78). At a conference in Munich, Germany, in 1977, he said, "The burning bushes, the smoking mountains, . . . the Cumorahs and the Kirtlands were realities; but they were the exceptions. The great volume of revelation came to Moses and to Joseph and comes to today's prophet in the less spectacular way—that of deep impressions, without spectacle or glamour or dramatic events. Always expecting the spectacular, many will miss entirely the constant flow of revealed communication" (Quoted in Graham W. Doxey, "The Voice Is Still Small," *Ensign,* November 1991, p. 25)."

When I was called to be a stake president, the Apostle who called me said, "I understand that you don't know very many people in this stake." I agreed, and he said, "Good. The Lord will have to call your counselors. You have one hour to pick them." He then handed me a list of names of people in a stake that we had lived in for only for a short time. I took the list home, knelt with my family in prayer, and asked the Lord, "Please, help me find who my counselors are." I then retired to a room by myself and began reading the list of names. As I read the names, I was just waiting. I know that sounds strange, but that's what I had to do, because I knew hardly a soul. I knew a few members within my own ward, but that was about it.

When I got to a name and felt good about it, I wrote down the name. Then I continued reading the list and waiting for another name. A second name came, and I turned in those two names as my counselors. This is not always the way inspiration and revelation come. But in my case and with the short time that I had, the Lord needed to call my counselors. I am truthful when I tell you I did not know who they were. I did not know what they looked like. I didn't know their jobs or anything. I had never seen them before. I just had two names.

I turned in those names and sure enough that night, after the Saturday evening session of conference, I got to meet my counselors for the first time. They were excited because they didn't know me and wanted to see who the new president was. We met in a room with this good Apostle, who instructed us and gave us great counsel. To me, that was a remarkable experience. It was not a smoking mountain or burning bush, but it was a remarkable experience. I will be forever grateful to the Lord for giving me those two counselors, for they were truly men of inspiration and wisdom and great counsel to me.

Speaking of powerful spiritual experiences, President Ezra Taft Benson said, "We must be cautious as we discuss these remarkable examples. Though they are real and powerful, they are the exception more than the rule. For every Paul, for every Enos, and for every King Lamoni, there are hundreds and thousands of people who find the process of repentance much more subtle, much more imperceptible. Day by day they move closer to the Lord, little realizing they are building a godlike life" ("A Mighty Change of Heart," *Ensign,* October 1989, p. 5).

Third, each of us can foster a climate in our own lives that makes revelation more easily accessible if we meet the conditions that the Lord has laid down. Some of those conditions include: maintaining personal worthiness, submitting our wills to the will of the Father, studying the scriptures and the words of the living prophets, and striving to be meek and lowly of heart.

The Doctrine and Covenants teaches us the following, "Behold, you have not understood; you have supposed that I would give it unto you, when you took no thought save it was to ask me. But, behold, I say unto you, that you must study it out in your mind; then you must ask me if it be right, and if it is right I will cause that your bosom shall burn within you; therefore, ye shall feel that it is right" (D&C 9:7–8).

President Harold B. Lee said, "It should not be necessary today for us to expect new written revelation on every point when we have these men [Apostles and prophets] thus possessed of that same spirit of revelation. A brief review of the past instructions of our leaders should only serve to warn the disobedient to continue faithful" (*Stand Ye in Holy Places* [Salt Lake City: Deseret Book Co., 1974], p. 283).

Fourth, we can further invite the promptings of the Spirit in our lives by applying the principle that the scriptures call importuning, or urging with persistence. Ways of importuning include prayer, fasting, repentance, humility, and submissiveness. Alma is a classic example of someone who importuned the Lord, in this case for his son. To Alma the Younger "the angel said: Behold, the Lord hath heard the prayers of his people, and also the prayers of his servant, Alma, who is thy father; for he has prayed with much faith concerning thee that thou mightest be brought to the knowledge of the truth; Therefore, for this purpose have I come to convince thee of the power and authority of God, that the prayers of his servants might be answered according to their faith" (Mosiah 27:14).

Fifth, when we try to force revelation or insist that it come in a certain way, we can easily be deceived. Even in importuning, we must not try to force our will on the Lord. The scriptures say, "Although a man may have many revelations, and have power to do many mighty works, yet if he boasts in his own strength, and sets at naught the counsels of God, and follows after the dictates of his own will and carnal desires, he must fall and incur the vengeance of a just God upon him" (D&C 3:4).

President Packer said, "It is not wise to wrestle with the revelations with such insistence as to demand immediate answers or blessings to your liking. You cannot force spiritual things. Such words as compel, coerce, constrain, pressure, demand, do not describe our privileges with the Spirit. You can no more force the Spirit to respond than you can force a bean to sprout, or an egg to hatch before it's time. You can create a climate to foster growth, nourish, and protect; but you cannot force or compel: you must await the growth. Do not be impatient to gain great spiritual knowledge. Let it grow, help it grow, but do not force it or you will open the way to be misled" ("The Candle of the Lord," p. 53).

Sixth, the Lord expects us to develop spiritual self-reliance. He taught that it is "a slothful and not a wise servant" (D&C 58:26) who must be commanded in all things. Revelation is not required for every aspect of our daily lives. Elder Dallin H. Oaks of the Quorum of the Twelve Apostles shared a humorous yet sad example: "The Spirit of the Lord is not likely to give us revelations on matters that are trivial. I once heard a young woman in a testimony meeting praise the spirituality of her husband, indicating that he submitted every question to the Lord. She told how he accompanied her shopping and would not even choose between different brands of canned vegetables without making his selection a matter of prayer. That strikes me as improper. I believe the Lord expects us to use the intelligence and experience he has given us to make these kinds of choices" ("Revelation," in *Brigham Young University 1981–82 Fireside and Devotional Speeches* [Provo, Utah: University Publications, 1982], p. 26).

Wouldn't it be embarrassing to be married to someone who must kneel at every aisle you go down to ask the Lord which brand of cereal you must eat that week. However, some cereals could use a prayer. Commenting on the same principle, President Packer said, "Things of the Spirit need not—indeed should not—require our uninterrupted time and attention. Ordinary work-a-day things occupy most of our attention. And that is as it should be. We are mortal beings living in this physical world. Spiritual things are like leavening. By measure they may be very small, but by influence they affect all that we do" ("Revelation in a Changing World," *Ensign*, November 1989, p. 14).

Seventh, revelation is often given in increments rather than all at once. The Lord tells us that knowledge comes a little at a time: "For behold, thus saith the Lord God: I will give unto the children of men line upon line, precept upon precept, here a little and there a little; and blessed are those who hearken unto my precepts, and lend an ear unto my counsel for they shall learn wisdom; for unto him that receiveth I will give more; and from them that shall say, We have enough, from them shall be taken away even that which they have" (2 Nephi 28:30).

Eighth, the Spirit does not cause us to act in ways that are bizarre or out of harmony with the sacred nature of God. Most of you are familiar with Church history and know that even in our own past there were some strange spiritual influences in people's lives. The true Spirit will not get you, at this point in your life, to leave your seat during a fast and testimony meeting and run around the chapel declaring the truthfulness of this gospel in a bizarre fashion. That is not the way the Spirit would be working upon you in a meeting. When the Spirit enters and touches our hearts, we should be at peace and calm.

The Prophet Joseph Smith described some early difficulties in this area:

> The Church of Jesus Christ of Latter-day Saints has also had its false spirits; and as it is made up of all those different sects professing every variety of opinion, and having been under the influence of so many kinds of spirits, it is not to be wondered at if there should be found among us false spirits.
>
> Soon after the Gospel was established in Kirtland, and during the absence of the authorities of the Church, many false spirits were introduced, many strange visions were seen, and wild, enthusiastic notions were entertained; men ran out of doors under the influence of this spirit, and some of them got upon the stumps of trees and shouted, and all kinds of extravagances were entered into by them; one man pursued a ball that he said he saw flying in the air, until he came to a

precipice, when he jumped into the top of a tree, which saved his life; and many ridiculous things were entered into, calculated to bring disgrace upon the Church of God, to cause the Spirit of God to be withdrawn, and to uproot and destroy those glorious principles which had been developed for the salvation of the human family. (*Teachings*, pp. 213–14)

I remember being warned about an individual who was visiting fast and testimony meetings in our area and saying some interesting things from the pulpit. Sitting on the stand in my ward one fast Sunday, I could see a man wandering back and forth in the back of the cultural hall. I didn't recognize him as a member of my ward. After an individual had finished bearing testimony, this man headed for the pulpit. He looked like the one they had been talking about. What would you want your bishop or priesthood leader to do at that point? I wondered, *Do I let him continue, or do I run down and greet him physically in the middle of the aisle?*

I decided I would leave the pulpit. I walked toward him, met him about halfway up, put my arm around him, and said, "I don't know you. Who are you?" He introduced himself as Elijah the prophet. I was so excited to have an angel in my congregation. I decided to take him out and visit for a little period of time. We visited and had a good discussion as the meeting went on. Later on, that Elijah somehow sneaked into the elders quorum. We should understand that when the Spirit speaks to us, it should not help us act in those strange ways.

Ninth, revelation that directs others comes only through properly constituted authority. This is a key principle to learn with priesthood leadership. On the other hand, personal revelation is for our own benefit and edification. I once had one of the good single sisters of the ward say to me, "You know, I feel very good about marrying this individual, but he doesn't like me. He has not asked me to marry him. There is another individual who has asked me to marry him, but I feel that I should marry the other person who is not pursuing me. What should I do?" Wouldn't you just love to be in such a situation as a leader and hope the Lord would help? Probably the right thing to tell her was that the brother in question needed to receive his own inspiration, which no one could force him to do and no one—including this sister—could do for him.

Elder Oaks said, "If a revelation is outside the limits of stewardship, you know it is not from the Lord, and you are not bound by it. I have heard of cases where a young man told a young woman she should marry him because he had received a revelation that she was to be his eternal companion. If this is a true revelation, it will be confirmed directly to the woman if she seeks to know. In the meantime, she is under no obligation to heed it. She should seek her own guidance and make up her own mind. The man can receive revelation to guide his own actions, but he cannot properly receive revelation to direct hers. She is outside his stewardship" ("Revelation," p. 25).

Elder Oaks also said, "We should understand what can be called the principle of 'stewardship in revelation.' Our Heavenly Father's house is a house of order, where his servants are commanded to 'act in the office in which [they are] appointed' (D&C 107:99)" ("Revelation," p. 25). Only the President of the Church receives revelation to guide the entire Church. Only the stake president receives revelation for the special guidance of the stake. The person who receives revelation for the ward is the bishop. Other Church leaders receive revelation for their own stewardships, such as an auxiliary or quorum. For the family unit, revelation goes to the priesthood leader of the home, with revelation also available to wives as they counsel with their husbands and to mothers for the benefit of children. Individuals can receive revelation to guide their own lives. But when one person claims to receive revelation for another person outside his or her own stewardship, such as a Church member who claims to have revelation to guide the entire Church or a person who claims to have revelation to guide another person over whom he or she has no presiding authority according to the order of the Church, you can be sure that such revelations are not from the Lord.

President Packer said, "I have learned that strong, impressive spiritual experiences do not come to us very frequently. And when they do, they are generally for our own edification, instruction, or correction. Unless we are called by proper authority to do so, they do not position us to counsel or to correct others" ("The Candle of the Lord," p. 53).

Tenth, personal revelation does not contradict or overturn established Church doctrine, policy, or procedure. Anything out of harmony with established principles should not be accepted. In 1913 the First Presidency wrote, "Anything at discord with that which comes from God through the head of the Church is not to be received as authoritative or reliable. In secular as well as spiritual affairs, Saints may receive Divine guidance and revelation affecting themselves, but this does not convey authority to direct others, and is not to be accepted when contrary to Church covenants, doctrine or discipline, or to known facts, demonstrated truths, or good common sense" (In James R. Clark, comp., *Messages of the First Presidency of The Church of Jesus Christ of Latter-day Saints,* 6 vols. [Salt Lake City: Bookcraft, 1965–75], 4:285–86).

Eleventh, we should not talk about sacred personal experiences too frequently. They should be shared only when we are prompted by the Spirit to do so. President Packer said, "I have come to believe also that it is not wise to continually talk of unusual spiritual experiences. They are to be guarded with care and shared only when the Spirit itself prompts you to use them to the blessing of others" ("The Candle of the Lord," p. 53).

President Brigham Young said, "Should you receive a vision of revelation from the Almighty, one that the Lord gave you concerning yourselves, or this people, but which you are not to reveal on account of your not being the proper person, or because it ought not to be known by the people at present, you should shut it up and seal it as close, and lock it as tight as heaven is to you, and make it as secret as the grave. The Lord has no confidence in those who reveal secrets, for He cannot safely reveal Himself to such persons" (in *Journal of Discourses,* 4:288).

When I was a stake president, a visiting authority shared something rather interesting: "From this point forward, the Lord will begin to reveal his secrets to you. How well you keep them will determine whether he continues to reveal them to you."

Somebody once asked me how we can have a great gathering in the last days at Adam-ondi-Ahman of thousands or hundreds of thousands of people and the public not know about it. I don't know the answer to that, but I do know this: on one occasion in a solemn assembly we as priesthood leaders were asked to keep sacred everything we were taught and not go back and share it publicly.

I wasn't thrilled at first because I had notified my stake that I was going to a solemn assembly and would give the instructions that I received. I was excited to share that. I took notes, but then at the end the prophet encouraged us not to do that. Not that anything was out of the ordinary or anything, but it was just a very sacred experience. When I came back that night, my family was waiting at the door. They were all excited to hear what I had been taught, and all I could say was, "It was a special experience."

When I went to stake priesthood leadership meeting, I had the opportunity of just saying nothing about the solemn assembly and teaching a whole different thing. All I could basically say to people was, "We have been asked to not share those sacred things that we heard." On some occasions you are welcome to go ahead and share; however, on this occasion we were asked not to, and honoring the request of the prophet we kept that shut and closed.

If you have the privilege to go to Jackson County or Adam-ondi-Ahman at that great gathering, wouldn't it be fun to be told, "Keep sacred what you experienced here." Then you could return home and say, "What a nice time we had." In your fast and testimony meetings, all you could do is say, "I just had a wonderful experience seeing the Church history sights." I don't know what is going to happen there, but if you are invited, I know you are the type that can keep a secret.

Twelfth, we must heed the promptings of the Spirit when they are given if we wish to continue to receive revelation. President Packer said,

> Now, once you receive it, be obedient to the promptings you receive. I learned a sobering lesson as a mission president. I was also a General Authority. I had been prompted several times, for the good of the work, to release one of my counselors. Besides praying about it, I had reasoned that it was the right thing to do. But I did not do it. I feared that it would injure a man who had given long service to the Church.
>
> The Spirit withdrew from me. I could get no promptings on who

should be called as a counselor should I release him. It lasted for several weeks. My prayers seemed to be contained within the room where I offered them. I tried a number of alternate ways to arrange the work, but to no avail. Finally, I did as I was bidden to do by the Spirit. Immediately, the gift returned! Oh, the exquisite sweetness to have that gift again. You know it, for you have it, the gift of the Holy Ghost. And the brother was not injured, indeed he was greatly blessed and immediately thereafter the work prospered. ("The Candle of the Lord," p. 55)

I bear testimony to each of you that this is the gospel of Jesus Christ, that this Church is built upon the foundation and the rock of revelation. I know this to be true. I know that President Gordon B. Hinckley is a prophet of God. I am so grateful for the Book of Mormon and the scriptures that teach of the divinity of Jesus Christ and His great work. I am especially grateful for the gift and power of the Holy Ghost that bears testimony to each and every one of us that this gospel is true. What a great and glorious work we have on the earth today.

Randall C. Bird is manager of seminary curriculum in the Church Educational System. A sports enthusiast, during his high school years he was named to the Idaho all-state teams in football and track, and he has been a high school coach in both sports. He also enjoys fishing, collecting sports memorabilia, reading, and being with his family. He and his wife, Carla, are the parents of six children and live in  *Layton, Utah. Randall currently serves as stake president of the Layton Utah East Stake.*

Watchman on the Tower

A few years ago I boarded a plane heading east for a speaking assignment. As I approached my seat, the lady next to me was joking around with some of the other passengers seated nearby. The accent was a dead giveaway. She was obviously from the New York area. Sitting beside her turned out to be fun because she had a great sense of humor and was very talkative. We chatted about all sorts of things and developed a nice rapport. She told me she was from New York City and had lived there all her life. She went on to explain the nuances of big city life to the little spud from Provo in a very kind and noncondescending manner. She was in her mid-forties and explained that this was her first time west of the Mississippi River. I asked her how she had ended up in Utah, and she explained that she was with a tour group that was exploring the West.

They had flown to South Dakota and gone on to Montana, Idaho, Wyoming, and Utah, visiting all of the national parks and tourist areas. They eventually ended up in Salt Lake, where they spent a couple of days touring the city. I asked what her impressions were, and she was very candid and complimentary. She talked about how beautiful the city was and how she had never seen such a clean place with people who were so nice, respectful, and friendly. I asked what her favorite attraction in Salt Lake was, and she immediately spoke about Temple Square. She mentioned that it felt really nice there, really peaceful. "Those Mormon people are really interesting," she said. I asked her what she had learned about the Mormon people, and she began to teach me all about the Mormons. She went on and on about her respect for them, how they were so dedicated to their religion, had walked across the plains after being persecuted so badly, how they lived such a disciplined lifestyle and cared so much about family. She sounded as good as the missionaries at Temple Square.

My new friend finally got around to asking me where I was from. I let her know that I was a Mormon, and she was a bit embarrassed but very excited to meet a real-life Mormon. I think she figured that they placed pretend specimens in a cage in Salt Lake and called it Temple Square, like a zoo, but that real people couldn't live like that in the world. She then asked if I would mind answering some questions about the Church for her. (Oh, twist my arm. Isn't that every member's dream?) A barrage of questions followed. I felt like a goalie in puck practice trying to get to all of them. Her first question was, Do we really pay ten percent of our income to the Church? I told her yes and explained to her a little about the law of tithing. I talked about the blessings and promises that come from obedience to that law and what a privilege it is to pay tithing and how much good it does for the Church and for other people. She went on about the Word of Wisdom and asked if we really abstain from coffee, tea, tobacco, alcohol, and drugs. From there she moved to the law of chastity and sexual abstinence, then to the importance of family, the Book of Mormon, temples, and countless other questions.

After a conversation that lasted the duration of the three-and-a-half-hour flight, she said, "I have one more question that I want you to answer for me." Her final question was a curve ball that caught me off guard. She asked, "What is it that makes you Mormons so unique and different from every other church?" (I resisted the temptation to shout, "Because it's true!") She continued, "I felt some things and I saw some things I never have before. What is the one thing that makes your church different and unique from all other churches?" I wasn't quite prepared to answer that question. A million answers popped into my mind. (Put yourself in my airplane seat for a moment. How would you answer that question?) I certainly don't know if there is *only* one answer, but that is exactly what she had asked me for. I don't even know if it is possible to reduce the gospel of Jesus Christ down to one unique thing, because of its vast beauty and complexity. But as I pondered what it was that makes our church so unique from all other churches, I looked at my friend and said, "I believe it is because we have a modern-day prophet living on the earth to lead and guide us." She said, "What do you mean?" I responded, "Just like Noah, Abraham, Moses, and all of the ancient prophets in the olden times, we have a living prophet who leads and guides us today. He is the mouthpiece for God and receives the word of the Lord from Him and then has the responsibility to share it with the rest of the world." She wondered where he lives, and I told her right in Salt Lake City. We talked about the role of a prophet and what he does. I shared a scripture mastery verse with her, Amos 3:7, which states, "Surely the Lord God will do nothing, but he revealeth his secret unto his servants the prophets." I explained that God has always used prophets to reveal His will to His people and that the pattern has not changed in our day. I then bore my testimony of how grateful I was for all the previous prophets and of what a privilege it is to hear from our living prophet today, President Gordon B. Hinckley.

Now whether that's the right answer or not, or even if there is only one right answer, I don't know. I am not in the position to make such authoritative claims. My answer was what I felt to be the most distinguishing characteristic between our church and all other churches today. Anything we have need to know or receive for our eternal well-being can be received at the hand of a modern prophet right now. Many other answers could be correct, but that was the feeling I had at that time. It really got me thinking about the importance of a living prophet, both for our day and in ancient times.

As part of Ezekiel's job description given to him by the Lord, he is taught:

> Son of man, speak to the children of thy people, and say unto them, When I bring the sword upon a land, if the people of the land take a man of their coasts, and set him for their watchman:
>
> If when he seeth the sword come upon the land, he blow the trumpet, and warn the people;
>
> Then whosoever heareth the sound of the trumpet, and taketh not

warning; if the sword come, and take him away, his blood shall be upon his own head.

He heard the sound of the trumpet, and took not warning; his blood shall be upon him. But he that taketh warning shall deliver his soul.

But if the watchman see the sword come, and blow not the trumpet, and the people be not warned; if the sword come, and take any person from among them, he is taken away in his iniquity; but his blood will I require at the watchman's hand.

So thou, O son of man, I have set thee a watchman unto the house of Israel; therefore thou shalt hear the word at my mouth, and warn them from me. (Ezekiel 33:2–7)

In Old Testament times, warfare was hand-to-hand combat. The most protected cities were the walled cities, which were the most difficult to conquer. The people would try to find the most strategic locations to build cities so that their enemies would have a difficult time overthrowing them. Cities were built on the tops of hills, such as Jerusalem, where it was difficult for an enemy to launch an attack. They would assign watchmen to sit in strategic locations on the tops of these walls to guard against any possible enemy intrusion. They could see far off into the distance, and when they saw a potential enemy approaching, their responsibility was to warn the people by blowing a trumpet or any other warning device and sound the clarion call in order to rally the troops in preparation to defend their city.

In this type and shadow, the Lord teaches Ezekiel his prophetic duty and expounds to each of us our responsibility to give heed to the warning call of prophets. When they see spiritual danger approaching, they sound the warning call to all the people that danger is on the horizon and they need to prepare so they may not be destroyed. He then lays out the battle strategy that will be the most effective in thwarting the enemy's onslaught. In other words, President Hinckley is for us a spiritual watchman on the tower in these latter days.

An excellent illustration of the importance of listening to prophets comes again from the Old Testament in 2 Kings, chapter six. Elisha is one of my all-time favorite prophets. He was quite a miracle worker and did many things to build the kingdom of God while he was on the earth. The basic story line of the Old Testament, as well as of the Book of Mormon, is that when the people listened to God through His servants the prophets, they prospered and were blessed, yet when they didn't heed that counsel great destruction (whether physical or spiritual) awaited. Because of the many miracles and great works of Elisha and his predecessor Elijah, the children of Israel were, at least in part, listening to the prophets at this particular time. Their big enemy was the Syrians. They had a much larger and stronger army than the Israelites, which is a tremendous advantage in hand-to-hand combat.

But the children of Israel were using Elisha the prophet to their advantage in this particular war. In verse eight of 2 Kings, chapter six, the king of Syria is taking counsel with his men of war and wondering where he should place his camp. He then chooses a very advantageous campsite. In verse nine, Elisha goes to the king of Israel and says, "Beware that thou pass not such a place; for thither the Syrians are come down." So the king of Israel warns his armies not to go by there, because that is where the Syrians are camped and they could destroy their army. Verse ten says that Elisha saved him "not once or twice;" in other words, Elisha's wise counsel saved the children of Israel many times from falling into the hands of their enemies.

The king of the Syrians becomes very frustrated, and he calls his servants and asks, "Will ye not shew me which of us is for the king of Israel?" Simply stated, he asks, Who is the spy, the double agent for Israel? He realizes that the children of Israel know where they will be located before the Syrians know for themselves where they will be located in these battles. His men know the situation and realize that Elisha is responsible for Israel's success, not a spy. His soldiers respond, "None, my Lord, O king: but Elisha, the prophet that is in Israel, telleth the king of Israel the words that thou speakest in thy bedchamber." How important was it for the children of Israel to hearken to the words of their prophet? What an advantage to have a prophet, especially in times of war! And isn't the war in heaven still raging on the earth today? The end to that story and war is incredible, but I will let you turn to 2 Kings, chapter six, and enjoy it on your own. I have sufficiently illustrated my point.

From modern Church history we have the story at Haun's Mill. The Prophet Joseph Smith warned those people to leave the area because of the impending danger, but they used their agency and decided on their own that they wanted to stay. One of the bloodiest massacres in our history then occurred: the Haun's Mill massacre. Seventeen Latter-day Saints were killed and another fourteen were wounded, all because of their failure to heed the warning trump from a prophet of God. Countless examples could be used to illustrate the importance of this principle. When people hearken—hearken means to listen and then obey—to God's holy prophets, they are blessed, yet when they choose not to obey, the results can be disastrous. It's the same for us today. When President Hinckley blows the prophetic warning, whether on moral, social, temporal, or spiritual issues, it is *always* in our best interest to obey.

Let me illustrate how important it is for us to give heed to our modern prophets by quoting excerpts from three different talks given in general conference that teach us powerful principles in regard to following our living prophet. Elder Alvin R. Dyer, an Assistant to the Council of the Twelve Apostles, shared this boyhood memory:

> To have a prophet of God in our midst, with the opportunity to follow his counsel and direction as he is inspired of God, is a compelling force. I remember, as a boy, attending a priesthood meeting with my father. I sat close by with my hand in his most of the meeting, especially since the speaker, Apostle James E. Talmage, spoke of the perils and deceptions of the last days which would try the faith of the members. One of the men in the meeting stood and asked Brother Talmage the question: "What will be the best thing for us to do in that day?" I shall never forget his answer.
>
> "My brother, see that you follow the counsel and direction of the prophet, for he is God's representative upon the earth, and he will know. (In Conference Report, October 1965, p. 19)

President Marion G. Romney, a former member of the First Presidency, shared this experience: "I remember years ago when I was a bishop I had President [Heber J.] Grant talk to our ward. After the meeting, I drove him home. . . . When we got to his home I got out of the car and went up on the porch with him. Standing by me, he put his arm over my shoulder and said: 'My boy, you always keep your eye on the President of the Church, and if he ever tells you to do anything, and it is wrong, and you do it, the Lord will bless you for it.' Then with a twinkle in his eye, he said, 'But you don't need to worry. The Lord will never let his mouthpiece lead the people astray'" (In Conference Report, October 1960, p. 78). That is such a comforting promise, to know that the Lord would never allow His prophets to lead His people astray!

President Harold B. Lee taught us an important principle before he was sustained to be prophet:

> We have some tight places to go before the Lord is through with this church and the world in this dispensation. . . .
>
> Now the only safety we have as members of this church is to do exactly what the Lord said to the Church in that day when the Church was organized [see D&C 21:4-6]. We must learn to give heed to the words and commandments that the Lord shall give through his prophet. . . . There will be some things that take patience and faith. You may not like what comes from the authority of the Church. It may contradict your political views. It may contradict your social views. It may interfere with some of your social life. But if you listen to these things, as if from the mouth of the Lord himself, with patience and faith, the promise is that "the gates of hell shall not prevail against you; yea, and the Lord God will disperse the powers of darkness from before you, and cause the heavens to shake for your good, and his name's glory." (D&C 21:6.) (In Conference Report, October 1970, p. 152)

What a fantastic promise! If we have the courage and faith to obey the counsel of our living prophets, the blessings that follow will be immeasurable, especially on issues that may not be as easy to follow as others for you, whether it is waiting until you are sixteen to begin dating or following the counsel to not have a steady boyfriend or girlfriend while in high school, to avoid pornography, to listen to your parents, to have the courage to dress in a manner that would be pleasing to the Lord and avoid some of the immodest or outlandish fashions of the day, or for every young man to prepare for and serve an honorable full-time mission. No matter what the issue, I know that I want those promises mentioned by President Lee in my life. I definitely want the gates of hell not to prevail against me and to have the Lord disperse the powers of darkness from before me and cause the heavens to shake for my good (see D&C 21:6). What tremendous promises are made to us for following the Lord's anointed!

I like to ask my students what they would do if it were announced on the national news the night before general conference that the Savior was going to be the first speaker at general conference on Saturday morning. How many people do you think would show up at the tabernacle? How many people do you think would want to be there in person? How many people would tune in and watch on TV, listen to their radio, get work off, or do whatever else was necessary to hear the words of the Savior? Then we read D&C 1:38: "What I the Lord have spoken, I have spoken, and I excuse not myself; and though the heavens and the earth pass away, my word shall not pass away, but shall all be fulfilled, *whether by mine own voice or by the voice of my servants, it is the same*" (Emphasis added). We learn from that verse that the Savior is the first speaker at general conference, He is the last speaker, and He is every speaker in between. Whether by the voice of His servants or by His own voice, *it is the same*. There is no difference. If He were going to speak at general conference, those would be the same principles, teachings, and doctrines that He would teach as well. I hope you enjoy feasting upon general conference as much as I do!

Before he became President of the Church, Ezra Taft Benson delivered a classic talk on the importance of following the prophet. The title of the talk was, "Fourteen Fundamentals in Following the Prophet." At the time, President Spencer W. Kimball was still the prophet. Following are the fourteen things that President Benson said are important in following a prophet:

1. "The prophet is the only man who speaks for the Lord in everything."
2. "The living prophet is more vital to us than the standard works."

3. "The living prophet is more important to us than a dead prophet."
4. "The prophet will never lead the Church astray."
5. "The prophet is not required to have any particular earthly training or credentials to speak on any subject or act on any matter at any time."
6. "The prophet does not have to say 'Thus saith the Lord' to give us scripture."
7. "The prophet tells us what we need to know, not always what we want to know."
8. "The prophet is not limited by men's reasoning."
9. "The prophet can receive revelation on any matter—temporal or spiritual."
10. "The prophet may be involved in civic matters."
11. "The two groups who have the greatest difficulty in following the prophet are the proud who are learned and the proud who are rich."
12. "The prophet will not necessarily be popular with the world or the worldly."
13. "The prophet and his counselors make up the First Presidency—the highest quorum in the Church."
14. "The living prophet and the first presidency—follow them and be blessed; reject them and suffer" (In *1980 Devotional Speeches of the Year* [Provo, Utah: Brigham Young University Press, 1981], pp. 26–30).

Brigham Young was famous for his never-ending support of the Prophet Joseph Smith. He serves as a great example for all of us in sustaining the prophet. President Harold B. Lee said, "The story is told in the early days of the Church—particularly, I think, at Kirtland—where some of the leading brethren in the presiding councils of the Church met secretly and tried to scheme as to how they could get rid of the Prophet Joseph's leadership. They made the mistake of inviting Brigham Young to one of these secret meetings. He rebuked them, after he had heard the purpose of their meeting. This is part of what he said: 'You cannot destroy the appointment of a prophet of God, but you can cut the thread that binds you to the prophet of

God, and sink yourselves to hell'" (In Conference Report, April 1963, p. 81).

How foolish and arrogant they were to think that they could replace God's chosen prophet with one of their own choosing. People with such thinking become false prophets unto themselves. President N. Eldon Tanner, a former member of the First Presidency, said:

> The Prophet spoke out clearly on Friday morning, telling us what our responsibilities are. . . . A man said to me after that, "You know, there are people in our state who believe in following the Prophet in everything they think is right, but when it is something they think isn't right, and it doesn't appeal to them, then that's different." He said, "Then they become their own prophet. They decide what the Lord wants and what the Lord doesn't want."
>
> I thought how true, and how serious when we begin to choose which of the covenants, which of the commandments we will keep and follow. When we decide that there are some of them that we will not keep or follow, we are taking the law of the Lord into our own hands and become our own prophets, and believe me, we will be led astray, *because we are false prophets to ourselves when we do not follow the Prophet of God.* No, we should never discriminate between these command-ments, as to those we should and should not keep. (In Conference Report, October 1966, p. 98; emphasis added)

While I was growing up, President Kimball was the prophet. He served in that capacity from the time I was around four years old until the time I was nineteen and serving my mission. He was the prophet that I had grown up with, he had signed my mission call, and he was my hero. He died while I was on my mission, and I was crushed. It was the first time I remember being concerned that the mantle of the prophet was changing. I remember my feelings as gen-eral conference approached. It was the first time that I could remem-ber President Kimball not being the prophet. Now we were going to sustain President Benson. I was on my mission, and I will never forget how hard I prayed and fasted to know if President Benson really was supposed to be the next prophet and mouthpiece for the

Lord. I knew that as missionaries we had to testify that we had a living prophet on the earth today, and I had quite a dilemma: I didn't know if President Benson was truly the prophet of God. But I will never forget the witness I received as he began his first speech as the prophet of God. My communication with the Spirit is usually very subtle and follows the pattern of quiet whisperings and feelings of calm reassurance, but not on that occasion. The Spirit overcame me and brought me to tears as I listened to the powerful words of President Benson. They entered my heart and my soul with so much intensity and fervor that I wept, and I knew without any shadow of a doubt and with a very personal and special witness that President Benson was the prophet of God and was chosen by God to lead His church at that time. I could then bear a powerful testimony that I knew we had a living prophet on the earth to lead and guide us because I had received my own personal witness from the Spirit that was truly undeniable. I've had similar witnesses about each successive prophet, President Howard W. Hunter and President Hinckley.

I bear you my witness that I know that we have a living prophet on the earth today and that we will be blessed when we follow the counsel and teachings given by our latter-day prophets and Apostles. They are men of God. They speak for God to the Church collectively, just as the Spirit will speak to each of us individually. It truly is a season for courage, and one of the key criteria to separate the wheat from the tares is the diligence the Lord's people give to the words of the Lord's prophets. It is my hope and prayer that each one of us will be diligent in giving heed to the counsel of God and find out for ourselves that President Hinckley is truly God's prophet on the earth at this time.

Brother Adams was an EFY counselor for four years and taught seminary in the Salt Lake valley for eight years, and he currently teaches in the religion department at BYU while finishing his Ph.D. He and his beautiful wife, Deanne, are the parents of three wonderful children. He loves all sports, outdoor activities, and most of all spending time with his family.

Using the Scriptures in Daily Life

I have spent the first twenty years of my professional life trying to persuade young members of the Church to read the holy scriptures. I work for the Church Educational System, and getting my students to feast upon the scriptures has been my almost-sole objective. I love the scriptures. I love reading them and likening them to my own life. My personal feeling is that they become the most meaningful when I do what Nephi said: liken them to my life. We read: "And I did read many things unto them which were written in the books of Moses; but that I might more fully persuade them to believe in the Lord their Redeemer I did read unto them that which was written by the prophet Isaiah; for I did liken all scriptures unto us, that it might be for our profit and learning" (1 Nephi 19:23).

I think what Nephi meant is that if we want to profit from the scriptures and want to really learn from them, then we must liken them to ourselves. That is, we must ask ourselves, How does this apply to me, with my problems, my concerns, my questions, and my challenges right now, not 2,500 or so years ago? As I have tried to persuade young people to do this for a few years now, I typically have gotten three responses from those who were struggling with scripture study in their lives:

1) "They're boring."

2) "They don't relate to me. This scripture is about something that happened 2,500 or so years ago to a guy wearing a robe and riding a camel. This is the nineties!"

3) "They're hard to understand, all the *thees* and *thous* and *it came to passes*. Why don't they just speak English?"

I would respond to each of those difficulties as follows:

1) There are no boring subjects; there are only uninterested people.

2) Usually, if you say something is boring, you are saying that you haven't yet been able to find out how that particular something relates to you. You have found no connection between you and that so-called boring thing. Typically, if you can see that something has relevance in your life—that is, that it relates to some concern or question you have—then you will no longer call it boring. When you are able to see a connection between something and you, the boring part goes away. Have you ever noticed that? It's kind of like learning to like a sport because you're interested in someone playing in the game, not necessarily the game itself. After a while, you find yourself liking the sport, not just the person playing it.

3) I was a full-time missionary many years ago when the earth was still cooling. Dinosaurs roamed the planet, molten lava covered the earth, the continents were all one land mass, and Adam was my first zone leader. Just kidding, but it almost seems that long ago sometimes. I was called to serve the people of Argentina, so I needed to learn Spanish before I left for the mission field. I spent two months in the MTC to help me out, and do you know how they taught us Spanish? We spoke it, listened to it, read it, memorized it, and carried a dictionary wherever we went. There was no magic formula, just hard work. How come you know what your name is? Because you've heard it, said it, and written it so many times. How come you know that three comes after two? Because you have counted so many things so many times that it has just become a part of you. Learning the language of the scriptures is almost the same: you just read them over and over and over, and that unique, precious language becomes a part of you. And by the way, when the Lord wants you to learn a language, He helps you. That's how I learned Spanish: a lot of hard work and the Lord's help. It's the same with learning the language of the scriptures: tons of hard work and a lot of help from our Lord.

But let's spend a little more time on item number two above. So many times people have a rough time getting interested in the scriptures because they don't seem to relate to our lives. We can sometimes see them as boring because we don't see a connection between what they seem to be saying and our own lives. Could I please try to offer some help in that particular challenge? Often in the Church we go to great lengths to tell people what they need to be doing, but we don't take enough time and trouble to tell them *how*. I might want very desperately to do something that is right and helpful, but if I don't know how to go about doing it I will almost surely fail. Let me try to explain how we could go about likening the scriptures to ourselves. If we could find out the connection between the scriptures and us, we surely wouldn't say they were boring, would we?

To help me understand how to relate the scriptures to my own life, I have broken the process down into four parts. I am sure that what follows is not the only way a person could liken the scriptures to his or her life, and I am sure as well that sometimes the Holy Ghost will help us liken a scripture to our own life without any steps or parts at all. Sometimes the application of a scripture will come immediately, by revelation, by the voice of the Lord coming into our mind and heart (see D&C 8:2–3) and helping us to know what that scripture should mean to us and what we should do about it. These four parts that I will talk about are only one way to look at the process of likening the scriptures to ourselves and to get us to be more aware of trying to find relevance in the scriptures, answers to our questions, and solutions to our problems. I would like to share with you what I have learned about how to liken the scriptures to my life. Get your scriptures, and let's get started!

Open your Old Testament to the book of Genesis, chapter 37. You are probably familiar with the story. Joseph tells his brothers about a dream he had in which he learned that his brothers would make obeisance to him, that he would rule over them. They hated him intensely before he said that to them, so just imagine how they reacted when he said he would rule over them. They wanted to kill him, but his brother Judah suggested that they make a quick shekel off the whole deal by selling him to some merchants en route to Egypt, who later sold him to Potiphar, an officer of the Pharaoh of Egypt.

Joseph apparently was a model slave, because in the course of time Potiphar made him overseer over his whole house. The Lord blessed and prospered that house "for Joseph's sake" (Genesis 39:5), and all was going well, sort of. Potiphar's wife took a look at Joseph and noticed that on a scale of one to ten he was about a 45 or so, and she said to him, "Lie with me" (v. 7). He said: "Behold, my master wotteth not what is with me in the house, and he hath committed all that he hath to my hand; there is none greater in this house than I; neither hath he kept back any thing from me but thee, because thou art his wife: how then can I do this great wickedness, and sin against God?" (vv. 8–9). In other words, Joseph said, "Look, lady, your husband trusts me so much with his stuff that he doesn't even know how much he owns. Number one, I can't do this to him. Number two, I can't do this to God, so the answer is no!" Mrs. Potiphar was apparently used to getting her way, because she was unwilling to take no for an answer. Verse ten tells us that she repeated her invitation to Joseph "day by day."

Finally a day came when no one else was around, and she went a step further. Not only did she say "Lie with me" to Joseph, but she grabbed his outer garment. Do you remember what he did then? Take a look at verse 12. The word used in the Old Testament is "fled." That wasn't a very sophisticated response, was it? He could have said something like, "I'm training for the Olympics, and my coach says that I have to be in by 8:30 P.M." but he didn't, did he?

Let's further analyze this story. You might read this account and say to yourself, "Well, that certainly doesn't pertain to me because that type of thing will never happen to me in my lifetime." Well, you don't know that for sure in the world we live in today. But let's say that you're right, that you never will be so blatantly tempted to be immoral in your whole life. Even if that huge assumption were true, we can still apply the story of Joseph to you. Watch how!

The very first step in the process of likening the scriptures to yourself is to find a general gospel principle that is dealt with in the story. In this particular story, which principle would you focus on? Scriptural stories often have several possibilities. In this case, we could talk about loyalty, couldn't we? Temptation? Morality? Obedience? Peer pressure? How many more principles are woven through this account of Joseph and his temptation? Hopefully a principle will jump off the page at you when you read. This would depend on what the Holy Ghost might want you to learn from this story this time through. You might read the same story three years later and apply it to your life in a different way, because in three years you wouldn't be exactly the same person you are now. You'll have different problems and different questions.

Just for the sake of illustrating the process of likening, let's say that as you read Genesis 39 the principle of morality is the one that strikes you as being important. Once you have centered in on a principle you're going to deal with, you are ready for step number two, which is to ask yourself, "How am I challenged in that particular principle?" In other words, "How am I challenged morally?" For some people, it's the books they read; for some, it's the videos they watch; for some, it's the conversations they have in the locker room. Anyway, you get the picture. This part is personal, and your moral challenge might not be the same as someone else's.

The third thing to do is to return to the story for some help or suggestions. Let's do that. What did Joseph do when he was faced with his moral challenge? Did he say to Potiphar's wife, "Well, we can do kissy face for a half hour, but that's as far as I go"? No! Remember the story, or look at verse 12 again if you need to: he fled!

Now we're on the fourth and last step in the likening process. Take the help from the scriptures and apply it to your moral challenge. If your moral challenge is the videos you watch, and Joseph fled from his moral temptation, what do you think you should do? I'm trying not to be preachy here, but it's hard. Do you think Joseph would see a video with only one bad part in it? Do you think he would say, "Well, they use that really bad word in the movie only two times, but otherwise it was great, and I was rolling in the aisles the whole time"?

Wow! Now, all of a sudden we're not talking about Joseph anymore, are we? We're talking about you with your challenges and questions right now, not a few thousand years ago. Talk about relevant! If you did step two really honestly and accurately and admitted to yourself in what way you are challenged morally, you are now face-to-face with what a scripture can mean in your life if you apply it to yourself. Sometimes that's painful because it means change on your part, but certainly you can't say anymore that scriptures don't apply to you, can you?

Are there other ways to apply this story to a human life? Certainly there are. Could individuals read this story and apply it to areas of their lives other than their moral challenges or temptations? Yes. This has been an illustration of only one way this scripture could apply to a real life.

Once you've thought through this story and what I've said about it, follow the four steps for applying scriptures to your life on your own. You may focus on temptation, or loyalty, or obedience, or peer pressure, or—the list goes on. The Holy Ghost will help you know the best way to apply the story of Joseph to your life at this time. Reread the story, think, pray, reread, find cross references that talk about the same principle you're focusing on, really work at it. In time you will find studying the scriptures so personally rewarding that it will almost become like eating or breathing to you. You won't be able to get through even a day without it.

I hope this has been helpful. As you study the scriptures in seminary, liken them to your life. They will become so much more meaningful to you. As the Spirit suggests to you how to liken the passages of scripture to your life, write down those thoughts and feelings in the margin of your scriptures, and act upon those impressions. Follow the advice of Elder Richard G. Scott of the Quorum of the Twelve Apostles. At a Church Educational System symposium on August 11, 1998, he said that if we want to learn to be led by the Spirit in our lives, we need to commit to live by this principle: I will seek to learn by what I—hear,—see, and—feel; I will write down the things I learn; and I will do them. Following that advice, we could hardly go wrong, could we?

John Perotti has worked for the Church Educational System since 1979 and for EFY since 1983. He loves playing baseball, playing the piano, writing novelty songs, watching old movies, and doing imitations. He imitates a piece of bacon frying in a pan; ask him to do it for you! He and his wife, Sheri, have three children. Brother Perotti graduated from BYU and later got a master's degree from Westminster College in Salt Lake City. He has taught institute and seminary in Utah, New Mexico, Colorado, and California, and he has traveled to more than half of the United States and several foreign countries to teach the gospel.

"Choose You This Day": Agency, Attitude, and Accountability

Little boys love mud. And a few years back, some elementary schoolboys in Springville, Utah, discovered the sublime joy of getting filthy dirty by going out for post-rainstorm bike rides through the muddy infields of Springville's finer baseball diamonds, which caused a bit of a problem for Bishop Alan Curtis. As the city recreation director, Bishop Curtis was in charge of keeping the ball fields smooth, raked, and in good condition. The mudfests which were such great fun for the neighborhood boys made for bad playing conditions on game day. Ballplayers were twisting ankles, grounders were taking bad hops into their faces, personal-injury lawyers were prowling around Little League games, so of course Bishop Curtis had to put a stop to this menace. He posted signs and got the word out. But one day, as the story is told around Springville, he caught an offending youth in the act, a lone dirt biker kicking up mud on the infield. Being a clever man, the good bishop handled this in a clever way. Instead of chasing off the boy or grabbing him by the ear and marching him to his parents, he crept into the announcer's booth and turned on the PA system. Cranking up the volume full blast, he spoke into the microphone with a deep voice that boomed out over the loudspeakers. The ensuing conversation went something like this:

Bishop Curtis: *Young man, this is the Lord.*

Boy (coming to a sudden halt, then slowly looking upward): Huh?

Bishop Curtis (trying not to laugh): *Thou shalt not ride thy bicycle on the baseball fields, henceforth and forever.*

Boy (whimpering in terror): I won't!

Bishop Curtis: *Now, go home!*

(The boy takes off, quite possibly breaking the land-speed record in the process.)

Now, can you imagine if the Lord really worked that way? If, whenever people were about to do something wrong, He spoke out of the heavens with a voice to shake the earth? Sure, it would make for some interesting situations.

Scene: A video store.

Kid #1: Hey, let's rent this video.

Kid #2: Hmm, I heard there's a bad scene in that movie, but, well, all right.

Thundering Voice from Above: *Thou shalt not rent that video.*

Kid #2: OK! OK! I wasn't really going to anyway.

(Later, back behind the high school gym.)

Kid #1: Here, smoke this.

Kid #2: Well, I know I shouldn't, but . . .

Thundering Voice: *Don't you smoke that.*

Kid #2: OK! OK! Look, Kid #1, I've gotta stop hanging around you.

Because you're bright, I'll bet you're already starting to get my point about why the Lord doesn't work that way. Can you see how it would pretty much destroy agency? And by destroying agency, it would destroy the whole purpose of earth life. Think about it: Could God bless us for doing what we were forced to? No. Could we grow spiritually and become more like He is by force? No. For spiritual growth, we need agency. In 1963 the First Presidency wrote, "Fear and force have no place in the kingdom because they do not produce moral actions, and are contrary to God's gift of free agency." If God wanted to, He could get everyone to *do* good, but no one would really *be* good. We'd all do what was *right*, but none of us would be *righteous*. Our actions would be driven from outside ourselves, not from within our hearts. The Lord is interested in our hearts. He wants us to choose righteous attitudes as well as righteous actions.

Agency

Do you understand agency? I heard one LDS teenager say, "Well, we're told not to watch R-rated movies, but we have our free agency." Hmm. Think about that comment for a moment. From his words, agency seems to mean "the freedom to do whatever I want." But agency is about more than our freedom to choose; it's also about the consequences of our choices. The scriptures say, "Ye are free to act for yourselves—to choose the way of everlasting death or the way of eternal life" (2 Nephi 10:23). Can you see the difference? Agency does not mean "I can do whatever I want and it'll be OK with the Lord." The scriptural concept is that God will not force us to choose right, but He will—and He does—tell us what is right and what is wrong. He tells us where our choices will lead us. No loving parent would do anything less.

Let me try to illustrate the relationship between choice and consequence. In my hometown of Ojai, California, there's a great little Mexican restaurant called Antonio's where they've created some spectacular salsa. It's not a wimpy, "made in New York City" recipe. It's a tongue-searing, eye-watering, ferocious little brew that I think Antonio's chefs have drawn straight from a fiery underworld river of molten lava. Even my dad, who pops jalapeño peppers like grapes and has a tongue of leather, gets little beads of sweat on his forehead after a few salsa-dipped tortilla chips. Well, our family once visited Antonio's when my oldest daughter, Kasey, was just learning to speak. She was sitting in a high chair watching all of us grownups munch away. I don't know why, but she thought the salsa was ice cream and decided that she wanted some too, so she began asking, "Ice cream? Ice cream?" We saw no ice cream around. When my wife, Lauren, figured out what Kasey was asking for, she of course did not grant Kasey's wish. "No," she said. "You won't like it. It will hurt you."

Kasey was even more insistent. "Ice cream! Ice cream!"

"No, Kasey, that's not ice cream, it's salsa."

She would not be deterred by semantics. "Salsa!" she cried, "Salsa!" She kept up the whining for several minutes, and finally

Lauren said, "If you want it that badly, go ahead, but you'll be sorry!" So Kasey had a spoonful of the killer salsa. For a few moments she seemed fine, but then the red-hot spices started to soak into her tender little baby tongue. A new concept began to occur to Kasey: the possibility that maybe her parents knew what they were talking about after all. Suddenly she was frantic: "Water! Water!" The next few minutes were uncomfortable ones for her. It took some time before she recovered. Thankfully, she learned her lesson about salsa, and I think most of her taste buds have since grown back.

Lauren knew what was best for Kasey and told her so. In life, the Lord knows perfectly what is best for us and what will hurt us, what will make us the most happy and what will bring us sorrow. He tells us through the scriptures, the prophets, and the whisperings of the Holy Spirit. We can choose either to follow or to reject the Lord's words, but if we reject them it's going to bring us misery every time. The consequences may not all be felt right away, but the end result of all sin is misery (see 2 Nephi 2:27). Someday when Kasey is older, she'll probably like spicier foods, and at that point we'll gladly let her eat them. Keep this in mind if ever you feel impatient with the Lord's timetable: He says no to some things at one point in our lives and says yes to them when the time is right. The scriptures say, "Trust in the Lord with all thine heart; and lean not unto thine own understanding. In all thy ways acknowledge him, and he shall direct thy paths" (Proverbs 3:5-6).

Attitude

Quickly take this multiple-choice survey:

1.(a) I love watching baseball.
  (b) I think watching a baseball game is about as exciting as watching my lawn grow.

2.(a) I think symphonic music is boring.
  (b) I am enthralled by symphonic music and have learned to appreciate the orchestra's exquisite range of expression.

3.(a) I think country music is boring and all sounds the same. It's all twangy, sappy stuff about girls that done ya wrong and pickup trucks.

(b) I agree with (a).

(Just kidding on number three! Ha, ha. Now, you country-music lovers, don't get so angry. Look, I play guitar, and I even learned one song by Garth Brooks, OK? So y'all just calm down there.)

Let's check your answers: Now, who is right? The classical music lovers or haters? The baseball fans or the lawn watchers? Well, with these questions, it's not a matter of who's right or wrong, is it? It's a matter of where we choose to place our interests. I've heard it said that there are no boring subjects, just uninterested people. We really do choose our attitudes.

People who say, "The scriptures are boring" haven't actually told you anything about the scriptures; they've just told you something about themselves. Those who speak unkindly about another person haven't really told you about that person; they've just told you about their own attitude.

When I was about seventeen, a new teacher was called to teach the Sunday School class I was in. She was a soft-spoken lady, much older than we were, and sometimes we didn't listen to her with much attention. I remember my mom one day making this enthusiastic and charitable comment about our new teacher: "Oh, she's one of the most Christlike people I know!" That impressed me. Because of what my mom said, I started to listen more closely in Sunday School, and I began to realize what a wonderful teacher we had. She was so kind, encouraging, and humble. I knew that she had a testimony of Christ, that she loved the Lord, and that she loved me too. She had a quiet but deep impact on my life. What would have happened if I hadn't changed my attitude? Maybe I would have continued sitting through my Sunday School class only half listening, making unrighteous judgments about this wonderful lady, and telling myself she was a boring teacher when the truth was that I was a boring student.

Got your scriptures? Look at Genesis 37. Joseph, the righteous son of Jacob, was hated by his ten older brothers. One day they made a plan to kill him, but at the last minute they decided instead to sell him to a passing caravan. That way, they not only got rid of him, they also made some money. (Now there's a dysfunctional family.) Joseph was taken to Egypt and sold as a slave to a man named Potiphar. Joseph could have been pretty discouraged at this point. He could have whined, "Why did the Lord let this happen to me? I've been trying to keep the commandments, unlike my brothers! What's the good of being obedient if it just brings you trouble?"

But Joseph seems to have chosen a different response. Maybe he said to himself, "Well, if I've got to be a slave, I'm going to be the best slave I can be!" I imagine him working extra hard around the Potiphar mansion, trying to be cheerful, treating his master with respect, doing his best to fulfill each assignment Potiphar gave him. Go over to chapter 39: "And the Lord was with Joseph, and he was a prosperous man. . . . And his master saw that the Lord was with him, and that the Lord made all that he did to prosper in his hand. And Joseph found grace in his sight, and he served him: and he made him overseer over his house, and all that he had he put into his hand" (vv. 2–4). Wow! From lowly slave to respected CEO of Potiphar Industries, Inc.

Well, what happened next? Enter Mrs. Potiphar, an immoral and dangerous woman. She began tempting Joseph, saying "Lie with me" (Genesis 39:7). Here is the great lesson of Joseph's righteous use of agency: "But he refused, and said . . .: how then can I do this great wickedness, and sin against God?" (v. 9). Notice his reason for refusing: not because he might get caught, or because he might get a disease, or because an unwanted pregnancy might result; not even because it would hurt Potiphar. Those all would have been good reasons not to commit adultery, but notice Joseph's reason: He didn't want to sin against God. Here's a young man whose relationship with God was real and personal.

Question: What kind of attitude allows you to have a real and personal relationship with God? When Joseph prayed, do you think he sighed to himself, "Prayers are such a chore," or did he more likely believe that prayer was a time for him to worship and really commune with his Father? The attitude we choose to have about our Father in Heaven determines so much about how well we obey his commandments. Is the law written in your heart? (See Jeremiah 31:31–34).

Back to the story: When Potiphar's wife couldn't get Joseph to give in to her temptations, she accused Joseph of assaulting her, and

Joseph was imprisoned. Again, we could hardly blame Joseph for becoming bitter or hard-hearted now. But he seems to have decided, "Well, if I'm going to be a prisoner, I'm gonna be the best prisoner I can be!" I imagine him helping out around the prison, cleaning out the cells, chatting with the guards, offering encouragement and hope to the other prisoners, and helping to keep order. Again "the Lord was with Joseph, and shewed him mercy, and gave him favour in the sight of the keeper of the prison. And the keeper of the prison committed to Joseph's hand all the prisoners that were in the prison" (Genesis 39:21–22). Wow! From falsely accused convict to honorary chief warden of the Egyptian Correctional Facility.

Turn to chapter 41. A couple of years later, news of Joseph's talents reached Pharaoh, king of Egypt. At a time of great crisis, Pharaoh looked at Joseph and asked his servants, "Can we find such a one as this is, a man in whom the Spirit of God is?" (v. 38). The Lord worked through Joseph to save Egypt and his family—the house of Israel—from a seven-year famine, and Joseph was appointed ruler of all Egypt, second only to Pharaoh himself. From humble desert nomad to viceroy of Egypt! All because of his commitment to a righteous attitude allowed the Lord to bless him: "The Lord was with him, and that which he did, the Lord made it to prosper" (Genesis 39:23).

We need more Josephs today. The world is in another time of crisis, and like Pharaoh of old the world is crying out, "Can we find a man or woman in whom the Spirit of God is?" You can be filled with the same Spirit and blessed with the same blessings as Joseph, but only if your faith is like his. "I obey because I want to; I choose to," said President Boyd K. Packer of the Quorum of the Twelve Apostles. "Obedience—that which God will never take by force—he will accept when freely given" (Quoted in *Teachings of the Living Prophets* [Church Educational System Manual, 1982], p. 45).

Accountability

A few years ago, a couple at the University of Alaska at Fairbanks decided to go inner tubing down a snowy hill on campus. There were warning signs posted forbidding this, but the couple ignored them. At the bottom of the hill, they crashed into a tree. Both the man and the woman were seriously injured. The woman died. The man sued the university, and the university was ordered to pay him $50,000. A magazine columnist, reporting on this and other troubling cases, made this observation: "Today the demand is for the right of anyone to do anything he or she pleases, and the right to be compensated for any unpleasant consequences" (George F. Will, "Our Expanding Menu of Rights," *Newsweek*, 14 December 1992, p. 90). Many people in the world lack an understanding of the concept that LDS young women stand and recite each week: choice and accountability. Those who really comprehend agency see that the *right to choose* is connected with *responsibility* for our choices.

One day we will stand before the Lord and give an account of our lives. God will not hold us accountable for things that we had no control over, but we will have to answer for matters in which we had a choice. Joseph Smith wrote, "Therefore, dearly beloved brethren, let us cheerfully do all things that lie in our power" (D&C 123:17). The story behind that verse is itself a powerful lesson in exercising agency. From the freezing pit of Liberty Jail, from the cell where he was being unjustly held while his friends and family were being mobbed and driven from their homes, from the shackles where he could do nothing to defend those he loved, Joseph was still doing all that he could: praying, receiving revelation, writing to encourage the Saints to be of good cheer! He was, when you think of it, so much like the other Joseph.

When you find yourself in a less-than-ideal situation, ask yourself, "What choices do I have here? How can I cheerfully do what lies in my power?" If your seminary class isn't going so well, what can *you* do to improve it? If relationships in your home could be better, how could *you* help? If you feel distant from the Lord, what spiritual barriers can *you* remove? (See D&C 88:63). To me, this is why agency is so wonderfully liberating: You are not a slave to your environment, though some in the world would have you believe that. You are not merely the product of your genes, which is also one of the world's teachings. You are free "to act . . . and not to be acted upon" (2 Nephi 2:26). No, you can't control everything that happens around you or to you, but you can control how you will respond.

When you understand agency, it puts you in the driver's seat of your life. Viktor E. Frankl, who survived incarceration in a Nazi concentration camp in World War II, wrote:

> The experiences of camp life show that man does have a choice of action. There were enough examples, often of a heroic nature, which proved that apathy could be overcome, irritability suppressed. Man can preserve a vestige of spiritual freedom, of independence of mind, even in such terrible conditions of psychic and physical stress.
>
> We who lived in concentration camps can remember the men who walked through the huts comforting others, giving away their last piece of bread. They may have been few in number, but they offer sufficient proof that everything can be taken from a man but one thing: the last of the human freedoms—to choose one's attitude in any given set of circumstances, to choose one's own way.
>
> And there were always choices to make. Every day, every hour offered the opportunity to make a decision which determined whether you would or would not submit to those powers which threatened to rob you of your very self, your inner freedom; which determined whether or not you would become the plaything of circumstance, renouncing freedom and dignity to become molded into the form of the typical inmate.
>
> . . . Even though conditions such as lack of sleep, insufficient food and various mental stresses may suggest that the inmates were bound to react in certain ways, in the final analysis it becomes clear that the sort of person the prisoner became was the result of an inner decision, and not the result of camp influences alone. Fundamentally, therefore, any man can, even under such circumstances, decide what shall become of him—mentally and spiritually. (*Man's Search for Meaning*, as cited in Marilyn Arnold, *Pure Love* [Salt Lake City: Deseret Book, 1997], pp. 422–23)

Your attitude will affect how much you get out of seminary, church, and school. It will affect relationships with your friends and family and your family yet to be. It will influence what kind of day you have today and what kind of future you have tomorrow. Attitude affects your whole life. My prayer for us all is the same prayer that

Moses had for the children of Israel centuries ago: "I have set before you life and death, blessing and cursing: therefore choose life. . . . [L]ove the Lord thy God, . . . obey his voice, and . . . cleave unto him: for he is thy life" (Deuteronomy 30:19–20).

Mark Ellison is a CES coordinator in Tampa, Florida, where he directs institute and supervises five stakes of early-morning seminary. He grew up in California, and served a mission to the deaf in Oakland, California and Phoenix, Arizona. He taught American Sign Language at the MTC and at BYU. He earned degrees in English and educational leadership at BYU. He is madly in love with his  *wife, Lauren, whom he married ten years ago in the Oakland Temple. He has four children. He enjoys running and playing piano and guitar.*

A Patriarchal Blessing: Your Spiritual Blueprint

Hey, let's go build a house! I have the land. You go down to the lumberyard and get the two-by-four studs and nails. I'll slip by Wal-Mart and get a bag of posthole cement for the foundation. Meet me back here in fifteen minutes, and we will have our house up in no time!

There's just one problem: I have no idea how to build a house. Do you? I know a little about the materials that go into its construction, but I have never attempted to put everything together to build one.

Are there instructions on how to build a house? Yes, there are instructions. These instructions are called blueprints. These plans show us how our house will look when finished and give us all the measurements, materials, and dimensions needed. Building a new home without a blueprint is like assembling a model car without glue: it is just not going to stick together. We may have all the components of the house, but without a good set of plans the outcome will not be what we envisioned.

The same analogy holds true for patriarchal blessings. They are literally our spiritual blueprints for building our mortal and our postmortal lives. In this life we need all of the help we can receive. Patriarchal blessings allow us to see ourselves as Heavenly Father sees us, with all of our strengths, weaknesses, capabilities, and blessings.

A Patriarchal Blessing Declares Lineage

"Patriarchal blessings," wrote the First Presidency in a 1957 letter to priesthood leaders, "contemplate an inspired declaration of the lineage of the recipient and, when so moved upon by the Spirit, an inspired and prophetic statement of the life mission of the recipient, together with such blessings, cautions and admonitions as the patriarch may be prompted to give for the accomplishment of such life's mission, it being always made clear that the realization of all promised blessings is conditioned upon faithfulness to the gospel of our Lord, whose servant the patriarch is" (Quoted in Thomas S. Monson, "Your Patriarchal Blessing: A Liahona of Light," *Ensign*, November 1986, p. 65).

A patriarchal blessing is a special blessing given to worthy members of the Church as approved by recommend from his or her bishop. It contains a declaration of lineage. You have descended through a royal lineage, even from Abraham, Isaac, and Jacob. You are entitled to the promised blessings of Abraham by the covenant line through his son, Isaac, and then through his son, Jacob, whose name was later changed to Israel (see Genesis 32:28). Israel had twelve sons who became the heads of the twelve tribes of Israel: Reuben, Simeon, Levi, Judah, Issachar, Zebulun, Joseph, Benjamin, Dan, Naphtali, Gad, and Asher (see Genesis 35:22–26). The Apostle Peter refers to these twelve sons as the "twelve patriarchs" (Acts 7:8).

Special priesthood promises were given to Abraham, generally referred to as the Abrahamic covenant (see Genesis 17:4–7; D&C 132:30–31), the total fulfillment of which will happen through the sealing ordinances of the temple.

The aged patriarch Israel gave what we might call patriarchal blessings to each of his twelve sons (see Genesis 49; *Teachings of the Prophet Joseph Smith,* comp. Joseph Fielding Smith [Salt Lake City: Deseret Book Co., 1977], p. 151). He also bestowed blessings on Joseph's two sons, Ephraim and Manasseh, the latter being the eldest. Joseph who was sold into Egypt learned that his sons, Ephraim and Manasseh, grandsons of Israel, would be counted among the twelve tribes: "And now thy two sons, Ephraim and Manasseh, which were born unto thee . . . are mine; as Reuben and Simeon, they shall be mine" (Genesis 48:5; see also JST Genesis 48:5–6). Manasseh should have received the birthright, or covenant, through Israel's right hand, but as Joseph's sons knelt before their grandfather, Ephraim at Israel's left hand and Manasseh at his right hand, Israel's right hand was guided "wittingly"—or deliberately—to the head of Ephraim. He crossed his hands and placed his right, or covenant, hand on Ephraim and his left hand on the eldest grandson, Manasseh. Joseph attempted to correct his father's error by repositioning his hands on the heads of Ephraim and Manasseh, but Israel refused and prophesied: "I know it, my son, I know it: he [Manasseh] also shall become a people, and he also shall be great: but truly his younger brother [Ephraim] shall be greater than he, and his seed shall become a multitude of nations . . . and he set Ephraim before Manasseh" (see Genesis 48:12–20). Many of you will be from this lineage, the lineage of Ephraim. The Apostle Paul testified of this event, "By faith Jacob, when he was a dying, blessed both the sons of Joseph" (Hebrews 11:21). Joseph Smith later recorded, "Behold, this is the blessing of the everlasting God upon the tribes of Israel, and the richer blessing upon the head of Ephraim and his fellows" (D&C 133:34).

It appears the first patriarchal blessings were given by Father Adam. The Prophet Joseph Smith recorded: "I saw Adam in the valley of Adam-ondi-Ahman. He called together his children and blessed them with a *patriarchal blessing.* The Lord appeared in their midst, and he (Adam) blessed them all, and foretold what should befall them to the latest generation" (*Teachings of the Prophet Joseph Smith,* p.158).

Ephraim's blessing is the blessing of leadership in the dispensation of the fulness of times. With leadership in the kingdom comes the awesome responsibility of the threefold mission of the Church: 1) proclaim the gospel, 2) perfect the saints, 3) redeem the dead (see Ezra Taft Benson, "A Sacred Responsibility," *Ensign,* May 1986, p. 77).

The tribe of Joseph, or in other words the tribes of Ephraim and Manasseh, has an important role in these latter days as illustrated by blessings given to the tribes of Israel by Moses as recorded in Deuteronomy: "And of Joseph he said, Blessed of the Lord be his land, for the precious things of heaven, . . . of the earth . . . : let the blessing come upon the head of Joseph. . . . His glory is like the firstling of his bullock, and his horns are like the horns of unicorns [wild ox]: with them he shall push the people together to the ends of the earth: and they are the ten thousands of Ephraim, and they are the thousands of Manasseh" (33:13, 16–17).

Now, let us examine more closely verse 17. The role of Ephraim can be divided into three areas:

1) "His glory is like the firstling of his bullock": Ephraim received the covenant birthright blessings usually reserved for the firstborn.

2) "And his horns are like the horns of unicorns": The horn is symbolic of "power" in the scriptures.

3) "With them [horns] he shall push the people together to the ends of the earth": Ephraim will push or gather Israel by priesthood power. This gathering is going on now throughout the world by our missionaries. The scriptures say, "Thou shalt magnify thine office, and *push* many people to Zion with songs of everlasting joy upon their heads" (D&C 66:11; see also D&C 58:45).

Elder Bruce R. McConkie of the Quorum of the Twelve Apostles commented: "As inheritors of the blessings of Jacob, it is the privilege of the gathered remnant of Jacob to receive their own patriarchal blessings and, by faith, to be blessed equally with the ancients" (*Mormon Doctrine*, 2nd ed. [Salt Lake City: Bookcraft, 1979], p. 558).

Youth of Zion, can you see why you are so important to the Lord? Most of you will receive your patriarchal blessings and claim lineage from Joseph through Ephraim by "the ten thousands," some of you through Manasseh by "the thousands." It is your mission and destiny to help fulfill the promises made to Abraham through the covenant line by helping to gather Israel. Your help in doing missionary work, strengthening your own membership in the Church, and performing temple work is imperative; these things *must* happen for God's full purposes to be fulfilled, and you are the generation chosen to do them.

Notice the responsibilities given to Ephraim in section 133 of the Doctrine and Covenants: "And they shall bring forth their rich treasures unto *the children of Ephraim, my servants.*" That's you and me! "And they shall fall down and be crowned with glory, even in Zion, *by the hands of the servants of the Lord, even the children of Ephraim.*" That's you and me! "And *this gospel shall be preached unto every nation, and kindred, and tongue, and people.*" By whom? By the servants of Ephraim; by you and me! (vv. 30, 32, 37).

My object in the first part of this chapter was to help you understand and visualize the importance of your patriarchal blessing and the part you will perform in the Lord's plan here upon the earth. Do you feel your importance to the plan? Can you sense more of a purpose and duty in knowing you are truly "youth of the noble birthright?" (*Hymns* [1985], no. 255).

Now, let's take a few moments and discuss patriarchal blessings in terms of what they are, what they are not, and how you would go about obtaining one.

What Is a Patriarchal Blessing?

"Your patriarchal blessing," said President Thomas S. Monson, "is yours and yours alone. It may be brief or lengthy, simple or profound. Length and language do not a patriarchal blessing make. It is the Spirit that conveys the true meaning. Your blessing is not to be folded neatly and tucked away. It is not to be framed or published. Rather, it is to be read. It is to be loved. It is to be followed. Your patriarchal blessing will see you through the darkest night. It will guide you through life's dangers. Unlike the struggling bomber of yesteryear, lost in the desert wastes, the sands and storms of life will not destroy you on your eternal flight. Your patriarchal blessing is to you a personal Liahona to chart your course and guide your way" ("Your Patriarchal Blessing," p. 66).

The Lord sees things differently than we do: "My thoughts are not your thoughts, neither are your ways my ways" (see Isaiah 55:8–9). "All things are present before mine eyes" (D&C 38:2). He is like the watchman on the hill: He has full vision. He knows us. Therefore, in patriarchal blessings the veil can be parted somewhat so that He might share with us something possibly about our pre-earth life, our earth life or even our postmortal life. He may counsel us on our weaknesses, strengths, attitudes, and abilities. Heavenly

Father may encourage, direct, or caution us in different areas of our lives.

The divine nature of a patriarchal blessing can be illustrated by parts of the patriarchal blessing of our dear prophet, President Gordon B. Hinckley. At age eleven, President Hinckley received his patriarchal blessing from patriarch Thomas E. Callister. While traveling to England to serve his mission, he reviewed these words: "Thou shalt grow to the full stature of manhood and shall become a mighty and valiant leader in the midst of Israel. . . . The Holy Priesthood shall be thine to enjoy and thou shalt minister in the midst of Israel as only those can who are called of God. Thou shalt ever be a messenger of peace; the nations of the earth shall hear thy voice and be brought to a knowledge of the truth by the wonderful testimony which thou shalt bear" (Quoted in Sheri L. Dew, *Go Forward with Faith* [Salt Lake City: Deseret Book Co., 1996], p. 60).

Conditioned upon Obedience and Faithfulness

A patriarchal blessing is *not* fortune telling. Fortune telling figures in the lot of chance, deceit, and fraud. It is a poor imitation or substitute for the real thing: the true power of God made manifest through a righteous priesthood authority, your stake patriarch. The Lord speaks directly through him to you. "An evengelist is a Patriarch," said Joseph Smith (*History of the Church*, 3:381; see also Ephesians 4:11; D&C 107:39). Patriarchs from the beginning have always been called of God by prophecy. The Prophet Joseph Smith's own father, Joseph Smith, Sr., was called by revelation on December 18, 1833 to be the first patriarch in this dispensation (see *Church History in the Fulness of Times* [Church Educational System manual, 1993], p. 122).

Elder John A. Widtsoe of the Quorum of the Twelve Apostles said, "These blessings are possibilities predicated upon faithful devotion to the cause of truth. They must be earned. Otherwise they are but empty words. Indeed, they rise to their highest value when used as ideals, specific possibilities, toward which we may strive throughout life. To look upon a patriarch as a fortuneteller is an offense to the Priesthood; the patriarch shows but the gifts the Lord would give us, if we labor for them. He helps us by pointing out the divine destiny which we may enjoy if we pay the price" ("Evidences and Reconciliations XLV—What Is the Meaning of Patriarchal Blessings?" *Improvement Era,* January 1942, p. 33).

The fulfillment of the promises and blessings given in a patriarchal blessing is determined by our obedience and faithfulness. Individual agency and accountability for choices will determine the outcome of those blessings.

"A blessing given by a patriarch," said President Joseph Fielding Smith, "is intended to point out the path which the recipient should travel. It should be given by the spirit of revelation and should be a great comfort and incentive to the recipient to continue on in faithfulness to the end" (*Doctrines of Salvation*, comp. Bruce R. McConkie, 3 vols. [Salt Lake City: Bookcraft, 1954–56], 3:170).

Preparing to Receive a Patriarchal Blessing

There is no set age at which you may receive your blessing. This decision is left to you and your bishop, with counsel from your parents. I received my blessing at the age of fourteen. I desired to receive it after an inspiring ninth-grade seminary lesson on patriarchal blessings by my instructor, Brother Coleman Jacobsen. The Lord gave me a spiritual nudge, or prompting, that I needed to prepare myself in order to receive this special spiritual blueprint for my life.

Your desire to obtain your patriarchal blessing should be prompted by a true spiritual interest and *not by curiosity*. Just because your friend is getting one or someone wants you to get yours should not be the motivation for receiving your blessing. Remember, the decision is personal. It is yours to make when you feel ready, but when you do feel ready, don't wait! There are things happening right now in your teenage lives about which you could use the Lord's guidance and counsel. There were important parts in my blessing which applied through my high school years in preparation for my mission. What if I had not heeded the prompting to receive it? I would have missed out on the Lord's wisdom and counsel through a very difficult time of growing up.

For example, a part of my blessing reads: "You have had the privilege of being able to attend some seminary classes . . . and will have more opportunities to attend seminary and institute." I was a four-year seminary graduate. I became a four-year institute graduate. Concerning seminary, President Ezra Taft Benson said, "Regularly attend seminary and be a seminary graduate. Seminary instruction is one of the most significant spiritual experiences a young man can have" ("To the 'Youth of the Noble Birthright,'" *Ensign*, May 1986, p. 44). I firmly believe I still fulfill this part of my blessing each day as I teach seminary. I am indeed having more opportunities to attend seminary.

Once I felt ready, I contacted my bishop for an interview. We discussed the importance of the blessing and the worthiness requirements. He gave me the phone number of the stake patriarch and encouraged me to set an appointment with him. I prepared myself spiritually by prayer, fasting, and scripture study prior to the blessing. I scheduled my appointment well in advance because the patriarch needed time to prepare and I wanted to be conscientious of his time.

I went to the stake patriarch's home for the blessing. In my case, my patriarch was Wilford J. Reichmann. He was my former stake president and the medical doctor who delivered me as a baby. He would later give my wife, Christine, her blessing too. So, as you can see, this is a most important man in my life.

He recorded the blessing on a tape recorder. In a few days, I received a typed copy of the blessing from him. A copy was sent to the archives of the Church. This copy is kept on file at the Church Historical Department. If for any reason I lose my blessing, I may request another copy by mailing three dollars to: Church Historical Department, 50 East North Temple Street, Salt Lake City, Utah 84150. I should include with my check my full name, date of birth, name of patriarch and stake, and approximate date of the blessing. I should expect about thirty days for processing.

Regularly Reading Your Patriarchal Blessing

It is important to review, read, and reflect on your patriarchal blessing often. We all need to refocus and reevaluate the direction of our lives. This meditation serves to remind us of our relationship to

God and His unconditional love for us, of our spiritual heritage, and of our divine destiny.

Some have reduced and laminated their blessings and carry them around in their scriptures, wallet, or purse for quick reference and inspiration.

President Benson encouraged the young women to read their patriarchal blessings often: "Young women, receive your patriarchal blessing under the influence of fasting and prayer, and then read it regularly that you may know God's will for you" ("To the Young Women of the Church," *Ensign*, November 1986, p. 82).

The question sometimes comes up: Should I let others read my blessing? This is a decision left up to you and your Heavenly Father. As you know, your blessing is personal. You should use great discretion in deciding who you will share it with. It is not only personal but sacred. You would not want to read your blessing to groups of people or even share and compare them with your friends. President Joseph Fielding Smith said, "Patriarchal blessings are individual blessings, sacred to those who receive them. It is not intended that patriarchal blessings should become public property" (*Doctrines of Salvation*, 3:172).

The recipient is encouraged to so order his or her life that the promised blessings can be fulfilled. As you read your patriarchal blessing, remember the blessing does not contain all the answers to our problems. The Lord knows we develop and grow stronger with the challenges we face.

Difference Between Father's Blessing and Patriarchal Blessing

"Patriarchal blessings may be given by *natural patriarchs*," stated Elder McConkie, "that is by fathers in Israel who enjoy the blessings of the patriarchal order, or they may be given by *ordained patriarchs*, specially selected brethren who are appointed to bless worthy church members" (*Mormon Doctrine*, p. 558; emphasis in original).

Your father is the natural patriarch in your home. The word *patriarch* can be divided into two parts: *patri* from Latin means "father" and *arch* means "chief." In other words, *patriarch* means "chief father." For example, I am the patriarch of my family. A father's blessing can be recorded in a journal or placed in a book of remembrance but is not sent to the Church archives. A father's blessing given by your father, or the patriarch of your home, can assist you with blessings of comfort, sickness, and inspiration. I enjoy the opportunity as a father to give a blessing to my children before they begin each new school year. It is always a most humbling experience to speak in the name of the Lord through this priesthood authority.

My sister-in-law Sandy Nelson experienced a wonderful father's blessing similar to Jacob's bestowal of blessings on his twelve sons. Her father, R. Gene Allphin, was bedridden the last year of his life, struggling to overcome the effects of emphysema and asthma. On August 5, 1984, he called all of his six children around him, four daughters and two sons. He gave them each a special father's blessing. Each blessing was tape-recorded in her father's own voice and then later transcribed for each daughter and son. Sandy was visibly touched by this experience. Recalling the significance of this event, she commented, "The Spirit was really there when, by the power of the priesthood, he gave me a father's blessing. Even now, when I read or play his inspired words, he seems so close." Her father counseled her to study the scriptures and keep reading them until she understood them. He encouraged her "to find your place as a mother in Zion and as a wife, to develop your talents, to understand your gifts in life and your place in life." Sandy felt this last statement applied to her two daughters, Erica and Nicole.

I have been so blessed by my patriarchal blessing over the years. I took it out during my mission and outlined it. As I read my scriptures and Church magazines or listen to inspired talks, I highlight things in my blessing which can add clarification and deeper insights. My blessing seems to meet my spiritual needs at whatever stage I'm at in my life. Some parts of my blessing apply to my life as much now as when I was fourteen. To this day I still remember vividly the powerful spiritual feelings I had when I received my patriarchal blessing. It serves as a constant reminder that Heavenly Father has provided me with a *spiritual blueprint* to build my life in such a way that I might fulfill all that I was sent here to earth to accomplish.

If you have not received your patriarchal blessing, I encourage you to prepare *now* to receive it. If you have already received it, I hope you will *read and ponder* its meaning for you. It is like your own divinely inspired personal scripture verses from the Lord through His chosen and ordained priesthood servant, the stake patriarch. May your patriarchal blessing ever be your *spiritual blueprint* from God as you build your eternal life.

Gary R. Nelson is a former high school and collegiate football and tennis player and maintains an interest in all sports, especially BYU athletics. He has been a sportswriter for two local newspapers. In addition to writing and speaking, he enjoys making his "animal imitations," singing, playing the guitar and piano, hunting, fishing, camping, bodysurfing, and spending time with his family. Gary and his wife, Christine, are the parents of seven children.

Effectual Prayer

I do not recall when or where I first learned to pray as a young Methodist lad in eastern Nebraska. I just knew that the act of praying never seemed to work for me. My prayers usually ended up with the feeling of talking to either thin air or the model airplanes that dangled from fish line attached to the ceiling of my bedroom. My earliest recollection of any type of prayer was the rote prayer my brothers and I would say by our bedsides while Mom or Dad stood in the hall and listened. It went something like, "Now I lay me down to sleep. I pray the Lord my soul to keep. If I should die before I wake, I pray the Lord my soul to take." This was not a very comforting prayer to me, but once it was said and my Christian duty done, I would jump into bed and say good night to my family.

The one time I remember praying for something from Heavenly Father was when I wanted a horse. I was only seven or eight years old, and I reasoned that living on a farm with plenty of hay and my hero being the Lone Ranger qualified me for having a horse. My dad would always smile and say no, so I thought I would take it up with higher authorities. I started on my prayerful quest by looking through horse magazines until I found the type of horse that I wanted. I would then cut out the picture of the horse and fold it ever so carefully. By the time I felt ready to ask God for my horse, I had cut out three different pictures of horses, folded them up, and hidden them under the pillow of my bed. Every evening when I went to bed, I would take out each picture, unfold it, and then hold it up to my bedroom ceiling and move it back and forth so that Heavenly Father, as He looked down on me, could get a clear picture of the type of horse I wanted. I would usually make some prayerful comments to God about all three of the horses I had selected, until I felt I had discussed and shown them sufficiently to the Lord. After my prayer with Heavenly Father, I would carefully fold my pictures back up and put them under my pillow. I believe I put my pictures under my pillow because I felt it might help in accomplishing my goal. After all, didn't lost teeth turn into money under a pillow? Years later, I finally got a horse. But by then my pictures were all worn out and I had stopped showing and praying about them to Heavenly Father. I reasoned that the new horse probably wasn't an answer to prayer because it had taken so long to come and it didn't look like any of the ones that I had shown God from my bedroom.

Soon I entered high school and faced the challenges that awaited me there. I had stopped saying the rote prayer at bedtime, and the experience with getting my horse left me feeling that my ability to communicate with God was somewhat lacking. I believe my desire to really converse with Heavenly Father earnestly began when I was a junior in high school with the sudden death of one of my dearest friends in a car accident. My mom seemed to sense my troubled spirit and the questions I had in relation to Mark's untimely death. She suggested one way to find answers was to look in the scriptures. She taught me to think of one question specifically that I wanted answered and, with this question upmost in my mind, to fan through the scriptures with my eyes closed. When I felt that I was in the place that would answer my question, I was to stop fanning and, with my eyes still closed, allow my finger to move across the page until I felt prompted to stop. The scripture where my finger stopped would be the answer to my question. I would then open my eyes and read what the Lord had to say to me. It never worked for me. My mom's suggestion, while being very sincere, left me with a bitter feeling toward God and weakened my already shaky confidence in my ability to communicate with Heavenly Father. This event escalated the already existing distance in my relationship with God, and the heavens remained silent to my broken-hearted questions.

Do any of these experiences sound or feel familiar to you? Have you ever said a prayer and, when you are finished, felt like it never made it through the ceiling of your bedroom? Have you ever felt that Heavenly Father just isn't listening or just doesn't care about you or the problems you face in your life? If you are similar to me, the question arises as to how one has effectual prayers, or prayers that really work.

My introductory experience with effectual prayer came during my first discussion with two Latter-day Saint missionaries, Elder Bybee and Elder Otis. They made a comment about prayer that has always stuck with me. They said, "Prayer is the means by which we can communicate with God, and revelation is the means by which God communicates with us." Communicate? It had seemed to this point in my life that all my communication had been one-way. Then Elder Bybee showed me a statement by Joseph Smith that sank deep into my heart: "It is the first principle of the Gospel to know for a certainty the character of God, and to know that we may *converse* with him as one man *converses* with another" (Joseph Fielding Smith, comp., *Teachings of the Prophet Joseph Smith* [Salt Lake City: Deseret Book Co., 1977], p. 345).

The elders then related some scriptural accounts on how the Lord conversed with us from the beginning of the creation of man. They showed me how God walked and talked with Adam and Eve, how when Adam and Eve were driven from the garden they could still hear the voice of the Lord from time to time. The elders went through a dozen scriptural accounts about how the Lord would converse with us, but none was as impressive to me as the experience of Joseph Smith.

As I have studied the life and teachings of the Prophet Joseph Smith, I have come to believe he followed an effectual prayer pattern that was introduced by Christ Himself when Christ spoke the sacred Lord's Prayer (see Matthew 6:9–13). In order for an effective prayer to be heard, one must first learn the manner and language that should be used in addressing our Father in Heaven. Because of my "Born Again" background, the manner in which I addressed deity was more casual and common. Elder Dallin H. Oaks of the Quorum of the Twelve Apostles spoke about the type of language that should be used in prayer: "The words we use in speaking to someone can identify the nature of our relationship to that person. They can also remind speaker and listener of the responsibilities they owe one another in that relationship. The form of address can also serve as a mark of respect or affection. So it is with the language of prayer. The Church of Jesus Christ of Latter-day Saints teaches its members to use special language in addressing prayers to our Father in Heaven. . . . The special language of prayer follows different forms in different languages, but the principle is always the same. We should address prayers to our Heavenly Father in words which speakers of that language associate with love and respect and reverence and closeness" ("The Language of Prayer," *Ensign*, May 1993, pp. 15–16).

When the missionaries commented on the type of words I used in saying my prayers, I wondered what the Lord expected of me. President Joseph Fielding Smith answered that question: "Our Eternal Father and his Only Begotten Son, Jesus Christ, should never be approached in prayer in the familiar expressions so commonly used in addressing human beings. The Father and the Son should always be honored in our prayers in the utmost humility and reverence. . . . The changing of the wording of the Bible to meet the popular language of our day, has, in the opinion of the writer and his brethren, been a great loss in the building of faith and spirituality in the minds and hearts of the people" (*Answers to Gospel Questions*, 5 vols. [Salt Lake City: Deseret Book Co., 1957–66], 2:15, 17).

President Spencer W. Kimball stated what words he felt should be used in prayer: "The presidency of the Church are quite anxious that everybody addresses the Lord with the pronouns 'thee' and 'thou' and 'thine' and 'thy.' Youth may feel that 'you' and 'yours' are a little more intimate and affectionate. Will you do what you can to change this pattern? It is largely in your hands" (*The Teachings of Spencer W. Kimball*, ed. Edward L. Kimball [Salt Lake City: Bookcraft, 1982], p. 119).

Now that we have learned the language we should be trying to develop and use in our conversations with Heavenly Father, let us examine the effectual prayer pattern that is outlined in the Lord's Prayer. This method of prayer has four simple steps. First we call on the name of Him to whom we are praying: "Our Father in Heaven" or some other equivalent, such as "Our Heavenly Father." This is how we let Him know that we want to get His attention and talk to Him. Second, we must thank our Heavenly Father for the things that we have been given by His hands. There is never anything that we cannot thank Him for. Third, we petition Heavenly Father for those things that are for our good and our development. It is good to think through the things that we want to ask our Father in Heaven to bless us with. It has been my experience that if we ask Heavenly Father specifically for something, we also better be able to state why we want it as well as what we will do with this gift once we obtain it. I also ask myself these four questions before petitioning Heavenly Father for a blessing: Is it for my good? Am I ready for it now? Is it fair to all others concerned? Do I honestly feel it is according to God's will? If this pattern of seeking specific gifts is followed, our Heavenly Father will know that we have spent some time pondering the petitions that we desire rather than just asking for a spur-of-the-moment wish. The fourth and final step is to close our prayers to Heavenly Father in the name of Jesus Christ, amen. We close in Christ's name because Jesus is our Mediator, Advocate, Savior and Judge.

I believe that Joseph Smith must have learned and used this effectual prayer pattern when he sought after the questions of his heart. The most obvious beginning to effectual prayer is having the desire to want to converse with our Father in Heaven. For most of us, the desire to converse with the Father is usually brought about by an event that occurs in our life that results in questions that only Father in Heaven can answer. In following the example of Joseph Smith, it would be well to have a clear and specific idea of what it is that you want to converse with our Father in Heaven about. Joseph was troubled about how to be forgiven of sin and which church then on the earth had the authority to forgive. His question was centered around which church would be the right church, would be God's church.

Once the question is solidified within your desire to know, the next step is to begin your own search for the correct answer and to gather knowledge. For years, Joseph went from church to church, listened to minister after minister, and asked several of the clergy his questions. We learn from his personal history that these ministers used the scriptures, but each had different answers from the same passage of scripture, which confused Joseph more than helped him. In his quest to gain knowledge, Joseph most likely turned to trusted friends and family members.

Stop and think about the last time you petitioned Heavenly Father for something you felt was important. How long did you search for the answer? Sometimes as youth in these microwave days, we expect immediate responses to our personal desires. We sometimes put our Father in Heaven into the role of our own cosmic servant, expecting Him to give us our answers according to our timetable and not the Father's. Then when the answer doesn't come in the allocated time, we feel that Heavenly Father doesn't care about us or isn't listening. If the answer to our questions isn't forthcoming, do what Joseph did: continue to search for the answers. Keep asking yourself the question, What more can I do? rather than the saying, "Haven't I done enough!"

Elder Neal A. Maxwell of the Quorum of the Twelve Apostles gave some insight into the reasons why it sometimes seems our prayers go unanswered: "Petitioning in prayer has taught me, again and again, that the vault of heaven with all its blessings is to be opened only by a combination lock. One tumbler falls when there is faith, a second when there is personal righteousness; the third and final tumbler falls only when what is sought is, in God's judgement—not ours—right for us. Sometimes we pound on the vault door for something we want very much and wonder why the door does not open. We would be very spoiled children if that vault door opened any more easily than it does. I can tell, looking back, that God truly loves me by inventorying the petitions He has refused to grant me. Our rejected petitions tell us much about ourselves but also much about our flawless Father" ("The Message: Insights," *New Era,* April 1978, p. 6).

President Boyd K. Packer of the Quorum of the Twelve Apostles gave some additional insight about petitioning Heavenly Father for obtaining answers to our prayers: "Sometimes you may struggle with a problem and not get an answer. What could be wrong? It may be that you are not doing anything wrong. It may be that you have not done the right things long enough. Remember, you cannot force spiritual things. Sometimes we are confused simply because we won't take no for an answer. . . . Put difficult questions in the back of your minds and go about your lives. Ponder and pray quietly and persistently about them. The answer may not come as a lightning bolt. It may come as a little inspiration here a little there, 'line upon line, precept upon precept' (D&C 98:12). Some answers will come from reading the scriptures, some from hearing speakers. And, occasionally, when it is important, some will come by very direct and powerful inspiration. The promptings will be clear and unmistakable" ("Prayers and Answers," *Ensign*, November 1979, p. 21). .

I like the statement, "It may be that you have not done the right things long enough." This tells me that I need to be patient and continue to keep the commandments so that revelation, when it comes, will be noticed. With this counsel in mind, go to people that you trust. Ask friends, parents, grandparents, aunts, uncles, brothers, sisters, bishops, teachers, or coaches and get insights from all these people. Take what they say and ponder their answers in relationship to the question that is in your heart. Expand your knowledge by a personal searching of the scriptures. Joseph Smith likely had read James 1:5–6 numerous times. But the day that scripture impressed itself into his life, Joseph had been pondering upon it throughout the day. As he read it again, it wasn't the scripture itself that answered his questions so much as the Spirit of revelation which comes to those who read the scriptures. That Spirit prompted him to action, to ask Heavenly Father himself for the correct answer.

I think we as a people oftentimes expect the Lord to answer our questions by saying it outright in a scriptural block. This can and does happen, but perhaps more often the searching of the scriptures brings a Spirit of revelation into one's life that puts one more in tune with the will of the Father and allows one to obtain insights and answers to the questions in one's heart. Eventually, the individual will have to ask the Father Himself if the knowledge obtained and the decision reached is in harmony with the will of the Father. It must be realized that the Father will not make decisions for one in matters that pertain to one's well-being.

The Doctrine and Covenants states: "Behold, you have not understood; you have supposed that I would give it unto you, when you took no thought save it was to ask me. But, behold, I say unto you, *that you must study it out in your mind*; then you must ask me if it be right, and if it is right I will cause that your bosom shall burn within you; therefore, you shall feel that it is right. But if it be not right you shall have no such feelings, but you shall have a stupor of thought that shall cause you to forget the thing which is wrong" (D&C 9:7–9; emphasis added).

Basically, you and I must make decisions from the knowledge that we have actively obtained and then take that decision to the Father to see if it is right. Joseph felt impressed to go into the woods to ask the Father his question. This example shows us that you and I should have our own "sacred grove" where we feel we can talk with our Father in Heaven without being interrupted or bothered, where we can focus with full purpose of heart. Joseph received, at this time, the First Vision, in which he met the Father and the Son. This type of experience will most likely not occur for you and me, but that doesn't mean we can't learn from the experience of Joseph. In the First Vision experience, Joseph conversed with the Father and Son, not just talked to them. The steps that Joseph took in effectual prayer brought him into the presence of the Father and the Son. The conversation that took place brought about life-changing experiences and the Restoration.

Using Joseph's experience as our guide, allow me to share with you a method that works for me in conversing with the Father. Start by kneeling by your bed as if you are going to say your evening prayers. For this conversing method to work properly, you must do it in the first person; you must actually put yourself into the situation and not view it happening as you would view TV or a movie. As you are kneeling, imagine in as much detail as you can what Heavenly Father looks like to you, perhaps sitting in a comfortable chair in His living room. Create in your mind's eye this specific Fatherly image. Once you have this image of the Father, imagine yourself standing outside a closed door which leads into the room. Now—this is very important—don't just see yourself knocking but actually put yourself there at the door and knock. Visualize in your mind the Father coming and opening the door. Feel what you would feel as He opens the door, and imagine what greeting He would give you. In my mind I see Him opening the door and extending His hand to take mine as He says, "Welcome, Cliff, it is good to see you again. Come, talk with me for a while." As He expresses this greeting, He not only takes my hand but pulls me in and gives me a hug. I visualize and imagine the feel of His arms and sound of His voice as if it were really happening. He then leaves one arm around my shoulders as He escorts me to a seat next to His, and we both sit down. I experience the Father turning His chair slightly to face me more directly, to be more intimate in our conversation.

Now this is where you begin to converse with the Father. In my experiences, I have the Father start the conversation by asking me how I am or how my day went. I imagine in my heart and mind what His voice would sound like and the feelings I would have as I sit there in his presence. I then answer His questions about my day. I go into detail about the good things and the bad things that happened that day. The spirit of making this conversation with the Father work is to imagine how He would respond to the things that you are saying and to have Him ask questions that you think He might ask as you explain your day. I also ask Him some questions, and at first I imagine or visualize how I think the Father would answer that particular question. Eventually, as I have gotten better at conversing with the Father and experiencing the conversation instead of just watching or listening to it, I have begun to receive insights and wisdom I know could not have been just my imagination or thoughts.

I believe that the more I converse with the Father in this manner, the more I develop a relationship that allows me to feel the will of the Father as he helps me understand the situations that I explain to Him. I pour out my feelings and frustrations and ask what I should do. I can often feel His love for me and receive insights that encourage me to try to become as He is and truly become His son in my actions or the solving of my problem. Eventually, as you do this type of conversing in the right spirit, it is my testimony that you will not only begin to feel the Spirit of the Father influence your life but that you will actually, at some point in time, literally hear the voice of the Father converse with you.

As your conversation ebbs to a close, perhaps you both stand and walk towards the door. As I say my good-byes after such a prayer, I will often feel the arms of the Father embrace me and give me a little hug. It always ends with the statement that He loves me and that He will be mindful of me until I come back later to converse with Him again.

Sometimes in my conversations with the Father, I do not always get the full picture as to why certain things seem to happen. But then I reflect back to Joseph Smith and realize that he wasn't given all of the knowledge of the Restoration during the First Vision. He was given line upon line, with enough of an answer to his question to bring peace to his soul. I have also learned that with particularly troublesome situations in my life, some answers do not come except with the added sacrifice of personal fasting. Sometimes we offer a ten-cent prayer and expect a million-dollar answer. If you want a million-dollar answer, you must be willing to give a million-dollar effort.

After Joseph left the Sacred Grove, I think he honored the effectual prayer pattern by following and implementing the last step. That step is in harmony with one of the most repeated commandments in the scriptural texts: to pray always. I believe Joseph continually prayed in his heart and his mind about the experience that he had in the Sacred Grove. So how do we learn the skill of always having a prayer in our heart and in our mind? I have learned that once I have developed the habit of picturing what my Father in Heaven is like and conversing with Him in prayer, the commandment to "pray always" becomes easier (see Luke 21:34–36; 2 Nephi 32:9; D&C 61:39; 88:126; 93:49). In fact, try the following little exercise in developing the attitude to pray always or always keep a prayer in your heart. Stop and think about how many times a day you say something to yourself or talk to yourself. Sometimes we are not very kind with the things that we say or think to ourselves. Now, instead of having this conversation with just yourself, imagine that your Heavenly Father is walking with you, and change the conversation as if you were actually talking with Him. Then every time you say or think something, you remember that you are conversing with your best friend, and thus the attitude develops of always having a prayer on your lips.

Joseph Smith learned throughout his life various modes in which the Father would converse with him. These modes are available to you and me as well. The most obvious manner of conversing with the Father is through visions and voices; however, this is rare for most of us. Dreams and promptings about how to solve a problem or receive an answer to a question are more common. Most common is an event that takes place or an idea or action that suddenly comes to mind or that burning feeling of surety or the calm, peaceful feeling in your heart telling you the answer is yes. Typically a stupor of thought, confusion within yourself, or a restlessness means the answer is no.

President Kimball told us that "sometimes ideas flood our mind as we listen after our prayers. Sometimes feelings press upon us. A spirit of calmness assures us that all will be well. But always, if we have been honest and earnest, we will experience a good feeling—a feeling of warmth for our Father in Heaven and a sense of his love for us" ("'Pray Always,'" *Ensign,* October 1981, p. 5). A good rule of thumb to follow when you are conversing with Heavenly Father is to listen for as long as you have talked. This allows the Father to converse with you through the Spirit.

This ability of developing a meaningful conversation with the Father will take some work and sincere effort.

It is my prayer and testimony that the Father hears and answers every heartfelt prayer. Sometimes the answers aren't always what we want, but answer He does. I challenge you to develop the ability to converse with the Father. As you do, may the truths that you discover in your conversations truly be a spiritual adventure.

Clifford Rhoades has been a seminary instructor for eighteen years and has worked with the BYU Department of Religion for three. He has also worked in Texas as the institute coordinator for UTA, TCU, and SMU. He currently resides in Idaho Falls, Idaho, where he teaches seminary. He was converted to the Church at age twenty-one and later served a mission in Ventura, California. Cliff and his wife were married in the Idaho Falls Temple and have four daughters. He has been a survival teacher, and he loves all outdoor activities. A former bishop, he currently serves as the stake Young Men president.

Decide to Decide

When I see a chicken, I often think of an incident that happened when I was twelve years old. We lived out in the country on a couple acres of land. During the summer were often played baseball in the backyard. If we hit the ball over the barbed-wire fence, it was classified a home run. The problem with home runs was that the ball would then be in the neighbor's pasture. No one wanted to go through the fence to get the ball because we were afraid that the neighbor lady would yell at us again. Whenever she saw us in her field, she told us to get off her land. I really don't know why she disliked my older brother and me. She had chickens that would often cross under the fence and come into our yard. Some thought that my brothers' friends who shot at her chickens with a BB gun were the reason for her disdain for us, but that was unconfirmed.

One day when I was outside, one of her chickens came into our yard. I reasoned to myself that since we were not welcome to pick up our ball in the neighbor's pasture, the chicken needed to go home. I tried to shoo away the chicken, but to no avail. Finally I found an old car's universal joint on the ground that could be used to frighten the chicken back across the fence. I thought that if I threw it close to the chicken, it would get scared and run home. I threw the universal joint toward the chicken. Watching the steel object headed directly toward the chicken, I thought, *You'd better get out of the way, you dumb chicken, or you're going to get hit.*

Now I don't know a lot about the anatomy of a chicken, but I do know that when a steel object weighing approximately four pounds hits the top of its right leg at a high rate of speed, it is not good. When this chicken was hit, something happened as the feathers flew. The chicken's right leg bent straight into the air, and it started hopping toward home on one leg. It was a terrible sight. I had meant only to frighten the chicken, but through carelessness I had mangled its leg.

Had I killed the chicken I'd have felt bad, but maybe I would have forgotten my stupidity after a while. But this chicken lived for months afterward. Every time I went outside and looked over at the neighbor's yard, I would see it hopping around on one leg, reminding me of my mistake. That incident happened many years ago, but I still have never forgotten it. Some would say I am a better person for making a mistake and learning a lesson from it. Why is it that I still wish I had not done it?

That day I made a decision based on an *impulse*, which is defined by one dictionary as a "sudden, involuntary inclination prompting to action." I've noticed over the years that many people ruin their lives by acting on impulses. Often immorality and experiments with alcohol, tobacco, and drugs began on impulse. These impulsive promptings are quite different from promptings by the Spirit. It is very important for us to know the difference. Be fore we pick up the universal joints in life, let's pause for a time to ponder decisions based on the Lord's plan.

Imagine your life twenty years from now. What kind of person will you be married to? What kind of job will you have? What kind of home will you live in? The kind of future you have may to a large degree be determined by the decisions you make in your teen years. President Gordon B. Hinckley said, "You can determine the kind of life you will have in your 30s and 40s by what you do in your teens" ("Messages of Inspiration from the Prophet," *Church News,* 30 September 1995, p. 2).

I believe the most simple and yet powerful counsel ever given for making decisions was given by the Lord. This simple formula will lead those who follow to happiness now and in the future. Decisions based on impulse are eliminated, and we become able to do what the Lord expects us to do. The formula was given by the Lord through revelation to the Prophet Joseph Smith: "But, behold, I say unto you, that *you must study it out in your mind*; then *you must ask me if it be right*, and it if is right I will cause that your bosom shall burn within you; therefore, you shall feel that it is right. But if it be not right you shall have no such feelings, but you shall have a stupor of thought that shall cause you to forget the thing which is wrong" (D&C 9:8–9; emphasis added).

I am convinced that using this simple two-step formula to study things out in our minds before taking action and then asking if our decisions are right would eliminate much of the sorrow and heartbreak in this world. Let's look closer for a moment at the Lord's formula for making decisions.

Study It Out in Your Mind

The Lord said that if we are to make wise decisions, we must study the options out in our minds. I believe he means that we must think of every aspect of a decision, including the potential consequences. Too many of us make decisions based either on impulse or on very shallow thinking. Often consequences are never considered in the thought process.

My father grew up in a family of eleven children, eight boys and three girls. My grandfather worked for a timber company, and the family lived in what was called a logging camp in rural Louisiana. My grandfather was not a member of the Church, and he had a drinking problem and a very bad temper. His children were afraid of him when he was drinking because of the physical punishment he would administer if they got out of line. My father and his brothers were close in age and did not have a lot of parental supervision. As a result they did not always make wise decisions. For example, there was the time when one of the boys grabbed a large poisonous snake by the tail and began pulling it toward their home. As the snake tried to strike at the boy who was pulling it, two younger brothers begged for their turn to pull it. It's a wonder they all lived to adulthood.

One of the memorable stories my father shared with me from his youth involves his brother Jarrell. One night the boys went camping in the woods near their home. As they prepared for the night, their mother told them not to take the .22 rifle with them. Of course, they were not prone to studying things out in their minds so they took the rifle anyway, against her counsel. Later that night the older boys went to find wood for a campfire. While they were gone, Jarrell decided to act on his impulse to shoot the forbidden rifle, but he did not want his brothers or parents to hear the rifle shot. Within a short time he came up with a plan that would allow him to shoot the gun without his brothers or his parents even knowing he had done it. His solution was to place his hand over the end of the barrel to muffle the sound of the shot going off.

Of course, the result was that he shot a bullet hole right through his hand. When his brothers came back to camp, they found Jarrell bleeding and crying. To avoid punishment, when they took him home they told their parents that he had fallen on a nail. But a visit to the country doctor further complicated their made-up story. He wanted to know how the nail had produced gunpowder in the wound. After several questions the truth finally came out. My uncle had made a decision based strictly on impulse. He quite obviously had not fully studied out the decision in his mind. Fortunately, the only permanent consequences for him were a scar and a lot of teasing over the years about this decision.

Do you ever make decisions without really thinking? Sometimes we tend to make decisions based on the first thing that pops into our minds. Often the results of this lack of serious thought can be inconsequential, while at other times it can result in disaster. By studying out things in our minds, we invite the Spirit to help us in our decisions. When the Spirit is present, we will make correct decisions. The scriptures say, "By the power of the Holy Ghost ye may know the truth of all things" (Moroni 10:5).

Ask If It Be Right

Sometimes we have another problem. We think we have studied out things in great detail in our minds, but in reality we have never thought about the potential consequences of our decisions. Other times we forget to ask the second part of the Lord's formula, "if it be right." Following is an experience that shows how far off some can get in their thought processes when they fail to use the Lord's formula for making decisions.

One night my wife and I were shopping at a local grocery store. While we pushed our grocery cart down the aisle, a store employee came running by, exclaiming that there was a man with a gun at the front of the store. He screamed at us to go to the back of the store. Thinking he was pulling a funny joke, we continued down the aisle. But with more employees running by, yelling for us to head for safety at the back of the store, my wife started following the others. My curiosity was piqued, so I continued to walk slowly forward to see what was going on.

I got to the end of the aisle and slowly peeked around the shelves. There in the front of the store was a man by the safe. He had one of the store's women employees by the hair and held a gun to her head. She was stuffing cash from the safe into a large, brown grocery bag. As this scene continued, a sick feeling came over me. I recognized the young woman being held at gunpoint as one of the members of my ward. I desperately wanted to help her but could think of nothing that wouldn't jeopardize her safety. I watched as the gunman yanked her by the hair and screamed orders at her. She was crying and begging him to let her go.

After she'd filled the bag with money, he began moving toward the front door. As the automatic doors opened, I saw several policemen with drawn guns. They began pleading with him to let the girl go and put down his gun. He hesitated briefly in the open doorway and then began pulling the young woman with him out of my sight. There was a brief silence and then several gunshots. I can't tell you how sick I felt at that moment. Suddenly the front doors opened again, and the young woman came running back in. When the robber reached his car, I later learned, he had pushed her away and told her to run. As soon as she did, the policemen opened fire and seriously wounded the young man. Leaving the store that night, I thought how close my friend had come to death.

The next day we found out that the young man who had committed the crime lived a short distance away from us and was renting a home from some very close friends of ours. He was married and had a small child. What thought processes had this young man gone through that led to his decision to rob the supermarket? Had he studied it out in his mind? Maybe he really had pondered the decision. Perhaps his thought process went something like this: I am not happy because my family doesn't have very much money. The family who owns the local supermarket has plenty of money. I wish I had plenty of money like they do. I know what I can do about my problem. I can take a gun into the supermarket and grab one of the employees by the hair and put the gun to her head and tell her to get the money out of the safe. When I have a bag full of money, I can take the employee out to the car with me and then let her go and make my getaway. Then I will have money and can be happy.

Is that what the Lord meant by studying it out in your mind? I think not. What did He mean? I think He meant to really study it out, including the possible consequences. I wonder if the young father would have gone through with the robbery had he really thought it out. I wish he had added a deeper thought process to his decision, such as: And when the employee is filling the bag with money, other employees will be running to the phones to call the police, whose headquarters are right down the street from the supermarket. When I step outside with the money, there will probably be several police officers with loaded guns pointing at me. When I let the girl go at my car, I will shoot at the police officers and they will return fire, possibly seriously wounding or killing me. Then they will arrest me and charge me with armed robbery, kidnapping, attempted murder of police officers, and resisting arrest. I will spend time recovering in the hospital and then spend years in the state prison. I will not be able to be with my wife and daughter. Instead I will live with hardened criminals. And the most ironic thing is that my family will have far less money than we had before my decision to rob the supermarket.

If this young man had *really* thought through the potential consequences of this decision, do you think he would have gone through the robbery? He could have saved a lot of time going through this thought process had he just asked one question. When the thought of robbing the supermarket came into his mind, he could have very quickly studied it out in his mind and then asked, Is it right? Obviously the answer would be no, it is not right. In fact, it is terribly wrong.

Of course, most active members of the Church never even think of things like robbing a supermarket. For the most part I don't think Satan wastes his time with such blatant temptations on us. His tactics on members of the Church are usually much more subtle. consider the following experience that a young woman had when she was in high school:

> I grew up in Salt Lake until I was sixteen years old, and I never considered watching R-rated movies as something bad. I would never do it in my own home, but many of my LDS friends did. Also, many of my friends' parents thought they were exempt from this counsel.
>
> It wasn't until my family moved to Kentucky that I really thought about the example that I set. I was the only Latter-day Saint in my high school. I made it a point to find out what movies my friends were going to before I went along. I even made suggestions for alternative movies when they picked R-rated ones. But then *Pretty Woman* came out. Everyone at school talked about it, and I loved the sound track. I wanted so badly to see it. I heard a group of my friends were going, so I went with them. We got to the theater and started to buy the tickets. One of my non-LDS friends said "Oh, it's rated R, and I don't watch R-rated movies. Do you guys mind seeing another movie?" What an example! I made a resolve.

Let's consider the process that this young LDS girl may have used to make a decision to go see this R-rated movie. First, her decision was not made on a quick, impulsive thought; it was made after much thought over a period of time. She had listened to the sound track and to the recommendations by her school friends and then made the decision to see it. Had she really studied it out in her mind? After all, she had thought about it for a length of time. But is just thinking about our desire to do something really studying it out? Did she consider the fact in her thought process that prophets have counseled us against seeing R-rated movies? For example, President Ezra Taft Benson said, "We counsel you . . . not to pollute your minds with such degrading matter, for the mind through which this filth passes is never the same afterwards. Don't see R-rated movies or vulgar videos or participate in any entertainment that is immoral, suggestive, or pornographic" ("To The 'Youth of the Noble Birthright,'" *Ensign*, May 1986, p. 45). Had she really studied out the decision in her mind, she probably would have never made the decision to go to the theater with the intent of watching it. Fortunately for this young woman, one of her non-LDS friends had taken the thought process one step further and asked if it was right to watch R-rated movies. Based on the answer she received, she had decided that she would not watch these movies.

Make Some Decisions Only Once

Many of the important decisions of life can be made before we are placed in a crisis situation. In fact, it is much better to make some decisions only once and to make them early in life. When we have not made a decision beforehand, we often choose the wrong way when a questionable situation arises. Consider the following experience of a young returned missionary who had not made a decision beforehand about R-rated movies.

The first weekend I was home from my mission in August 1992, I got together with a group of old friends to go out and talk about the good old times and have some fun. We ended up going out to get a video and returned to a friend's house to watch it. It never even crossed my mind to ask what the video was rated because I hadn't seen a movie for two years and I just assumed it would be good because all the other guys I was with were returned missionaries. When we started to watch the movie, a younger sister of one of my friends came in and asked the name of the movie and was shocked because it was rated R. She then went on to say that it disappointed her that a group of RMs would watch R-rated movies. When this happened it really hit me hard, and I knew I had to make a decision. I could either continue on the path I was following before my mission, or I could apply what I had learned on my mission and not watch R-rated movies. I decided not to watch R-rated movies ever again. Since then I have received a lot of pressure from friends and fellow students, but I have made a commitment.

We don't have to wait until we are placed in a tempting situation to go through the Lord's decision formula. The younger sister of this returned missionary's friend had made her decision early in life to not watch R-rated movies. We all can predetermine many of our decisions by studying out things in our minds before being placed in the situation. President Spencer W. Kimball said:

> One of the basic tasks for each individual is the making of decisions. A dozen times a day we come to a fork in the road and must decide which way we will go. . . . It is important to get our ultimate objectives clearly in mind so that we do not become distracted at each fork in the road by the irrelevant questions: Which is the easier or more pleasant way? or, Which way are others going?
>
> Right decisions are easiest to make when we make them well in advance, having ultimate objectives in mind; this saves a lot of anguish at the fork, when we're tired and sorely tempted.
>
> When I was young, I made up my mind unalterably that I would never taste tea, coffee, tobacco, or liquor. I found that this rigid determination saved me many times throughout my varied experiences. There were many occasions when I could have sipped or touched or sampled, but the unalterable determination firmly established gave me good reason and good strength to resist.
>
> The time to decide on a mission is long before it becomes a matter of choosing between a mission and an athletic scholarship. The time to decide on temple marriage is before one has become attached to a boyfriend or girl friend who does not share that objective. The time to decide on a policy of strict honesty is before the store clerk gives you too much change. The time to decide against using drugs is before a friend you like teases you for being afraid or pious. The time to decide that we will settle for nothing less than an opportunity to live eternally with our Father is now, so that every choice we make will be affected by our determination to let nothing interfere with attaining that ultimate goal. ("The Message: Decisions: Why It's Important to Make Some Now," *New Era*, April 1971, p. 2)

President Kimball also taught, "Make certain decisions only once. . . . We can make a single decision about certain things that we will incorporate in our lives and then make them ours—without having to brood and redecide a hundred times what it is we will do and what we will not do" ("Boys Need Heroes Close By," *Ensign*, May 1976, p. 46).

The following is an example of one young man's decision to remain morally clean during the dating years. He made two lists:

This I Will Do
1. I will date only those who are worthy Church members striving for a temple marriage.
2. I will return my date home as clean as when she left.
3. I will attend only activities that meet Church standards.
4. After every date, I will discuss my activities with my parents.
5. I will get up and run like Joseph of old if I am ever tempted to be immoral.
6. I will tell both my parents and my date's parents exactly where we will be and when we will be home. I will call if our plans change.
7. I will treat every girl I go out with the way I would want my future wife to be treated by those she dates.

This I Will Not Do
1. I will never be alone with a member of the opposite sex in places where unwholesome things could happen.
2. I will not date until I am sixteen years old.
3. I will never do anything with a member of the opposite sex that I would be embarrassed to share with my parents or Church leaders.
4. I will not "go steady" in my teen years.
5. I will not kiss anyone in casual dating.
6. I will not single date until I am ready for serious courtship and marriage.
7. I will not watch R-rated movies or any movie or television program, read any books, or listen to any music that would place immoral thoughts in my mind.

I believe that one day such a young man will kneel across the altar from an equally moral young woman in the house of the Lord.

Once certain decisions are made, they become the standard by which individual questions are answered. When hard questions arise, the answers are already predetermined. Little decisions made early in life often have tremendous impact in later life when the winds of temptation and adversity come with fury: "Behold also the ships, which though they be so great, and are driven of fierce winds, yet are they turned about with a very small helm" (James 3:4).

Over the years I have had the opportunity to work with many outstanding young people. Some stick out in my memory more than others. One I well remember is Monica. She played the piano, was a straight-A student in high school, and never missed a day of early-morning seminary in four years even though the starting time was 5:55 A.M. She was also very pretty. After graduating from high school, she went away to college but eventually came back and married a returned missionary from her home area. After her marriage she spoke to some young men and young women at a youth standards night. She was the perfect one to speak because she had maintained such high standards during her teenage years.

Monica said that when she was a young girl she made a vow that she would follow the prophets. This is not an easy thing to do when it applies to dating and other standards that people in our society have different views about. She said that when she was fourteen and fifteen, she was asked out on dates multiple times. She had an easy way out during that time of her life because all she had to say was that she could not date until age sixteen. The biggest event during her eighth-grade year was the end-of-the-year banquet, a formal dinner dance. Monica was one of only a few girls who attended this special event without a date. Even some of the LDS girls met their friends at the banquet, exchanged corsages and boutonnieres, and spent the evening exclusively with each other. It was a very hard night for Monica.

When she turned sixteen, she discovered a problem she had not fully anticipated. Although the phone continued to ring, most of the young men on the line were not members of the Church and did not have the high moral standards she was seeking. She took a stand and decided to follow the prophets, even though she attended a large, predominately nonmember high school.

Then the phone quit ringing, and the young girl who had decided to follow the prophets' guidelines had very few dates. She said it wasn't so bad, though, since she was able to work on goals such as sewing, cooking, making good grades, reading the scriptures, and obtaining her Young Womanhood Recognition award. She was also an officer for the dance team. Monica did well enough in high school to receive a scholarship to Brigham Young University. After a year at BYU she met a young, good-looking returned missionary. They courted and then began a new life together after their marriage in the Washington (D.C.) Temple.

She next told the youth that as she had knelt across the altar of the temple, she thought of the eighth-grade banquet and how hard that night was and all the other nights she sat at home. But then came her point. She said, "I want to tell all of you here that when I knelt across the altar at the Washington (D.C.) Temple and looked into the eyes of a worthy priesthood holder and heard 'married for time and eternity,' I knew it was all worth it!"

As a teenager Monica decided the life she would have in her thirties and forties, just as President Gordon B. Hinckley said we could do. If you haven't decided on a course for your life, then why not follow the counsel of Joshua: "Choose you this day whom ye will serve" (Joshua 24:15). Or as President Spencer W. Kimball said, "If you have not done so yet, decide to decide" ("Boys Need Heroes Close By," p. 46).

Over the course of many years, I have had the opportunity to make many decisions and to observe the decisions of others. I have read books about the decision-making process and heard many talks on the subject. If I were asked to share the best advice I could come up with on the subject, I would simply say, "Study it out in your mind" and ask Heavenly Father if it be right. I'm confident that if we would follow this simple guideline set forth by the Lord, we would live lives of great happiness. I'm also convinced that the best time to decide to live a righteous life is during the teenage years. I hope that you will decide today the kind of life you will live and that you will always use the Lord's formula when faced with future decisions.

Randal Wright was born and raised in Texas and currently serves as the institute director for the Church Educational System. He has a Ph.D. in family studies from BYU and has done extensive research on the impact of electronic media on adolescents. He has also written articles for several magazines and published five books. He loves basketball, music, books, red velvet cake, and being at  *home with his family. He and his wife, Wendy, are the parents of five children and reside in Austin, Texas.*

Why We Need Christ

When I was in Arizona teaching seminary and institute, I had a strange experience one evening. A friend whose children I had had the opportunity of teaching asked if I would come over to his house for a discussion with some people that he had recently met. I went over, and it didn't take long to see that these people weren't really, shall we say, pro-Mormon. As a matter of fact, they kept telling me that I wasn't even a Christian. I couldn't believe it. Basically, they were absolutely sure that unless I were to change what I believed and accept Christ, I was headed straight for hell. *How pleasant*, I thought.

Some years ago I read an article in *Newsweek* magazine titled, "What Mormons Believe." As I read through it, I was amazed at one particular statement; see if you agree with it: "Unlike orthodox Christians, Mormons believe that men are born free of sin and *earn their way to godhood* by the proper exercise of free will, rather than through the grace of Jesus Christ. Thus Jesus' suffering and death in the Mormon view were brotherly acts of compassion, but they do not atone for the sins of others" (1 September 1980, p. 68; emphasis added).

What? I couldn't believe it. Later, someone wrote to ask the author of the *Newsweek* article how he could say that about the Mormons. He responded basically that he was not trying to describe what the Mormon Church teaches but what the members of the Church actually believe.

So I ask: What do we believe about Christ? Are we Christian? Do we really understand why we need the Savior?

When President Gordon B. Hinckley finally receives his final judgment, where do you think he will go, the celestial, terrestrial, or telestial kingdom? When Hitler receives his final judgment, which kingdom will he receive? You probably put President Hinckley in the celestial kingdom, and Hitler, at best, in the telestial.

Now, let's try it again, but instead let's change one thing about the plan of salvation. Let's simply say that Jesus never accepted to become our Savior, and therefore there was no Atonement made for each of us. In this case, where would President Hinckley go? Could he still inherit the celestial kingdom? What about Hitler?

President Ezra Taft Benson said, "Just as a man does not really desire food until he is hungry, so he does not desire the salvation of Christ until he knows why he needs Christ. No one adequately and properly knows why he needs Christ until he understands and accepts the doctrine of the Fall and its effect upon all mankind. And no other book in the world explains this vital doctrine nearly as well as the Book of Mormon" ("The Book of Mormon and the Doctrine and Covenants," *Ensign*, May 1987, p. 85).

What effect does the Fall of Adam have on all of us? When Adam partook of the fruit in the Garden of Eden, two kinds of death were introduced into the world: physical death and spiritual death. Physical death is the separation of our body and spirit. Spiritual death is our separation from the presence of God. Both of these deaths come upon all of us without exception.

In the Book of Mormon we read:

> For as death hath passed upon all men, . . . there must needs be a power of resurrection, and the resurrection must needs come unto man by reason of the fall [remember, we will all die physically someday and will need to be resurrected]; and the fall came by reason of transgression [Adam and Eve]; and because man became fallen they were cut off from the presence of the Lord [spiritual death].
>
> Wherefore, it must needs be an infinite atonement—save [unless] it should be an infinite atonement this corruption [our mortal bodies] could not put on incorruption [be resurrected]. Wherefore, the first judgment

which came upon man [because of the Fall of Adam] must needs have remained to an endless duration. And if so, this flesh must have laid down to rot and to crumble to its mother earth, to rise no more.

O the wisdom of God, his mercy and grace! For behold, if the flesh should rise no more our spirits *must* [not might!] become subject to that angel who fell from before the presence of the Eternal God, and became the devil, to rise no more.

And our spirits must [again, not might!] have become like unto him [Satan], and we become devils, angels to a devil." (2 Nephi 9:6–9; emphasis added)

Did you catch that? In other words, without the Atonement all of us would become little devils. You see, without the Atonement, there would be no resurrection. All of us, including the Hinckleys and the Hitlers, would remain without our glorified bodies forever. Who can bring himself back to life? No one except Christ.

Let me repeat, without the Atonement all men, women, and children would forever be lost. All would end up with Satan.

Now, with the Atonement, what happens to the effects of the Fall? How many people will be resurrected? The Apostle Paul simply says, "As in Adam all die, even so in Christ shall all be made alive" (1 Corinthians 15:22). The answer? One hundred percent. Anyone who came to earth and received a body, no matter how evil or good, gets a resurrected body. The physical death caused by Adam is unconditionally overcome by the Atonement of Christ.

What about the spiritual death, or separation from God, caused by Adam?

Notice Helaman 14:15–17: "For behold, he [Christ] surely must die that salvation may come; yea, . . . to bring to pass the resurrection of the dead, that thereby men may be brought into the presence of the Lord. Yea, behold, this death bringeth to pass the resurrection, and redeemeth all mankind from the first death—that spiritual death; for all mankind, by the fall of Adam being cut off from the presence of the Lord, are considered as dead, both as to things temporal [or physical] and to things spiritual. But behold, the resurrection of Christ redeemeth mankind, yea, even all mankind, and bringeth them back into the presence of the Lord."

Through the Atonement, our physical death is overcome by the knowledge that our bodies will be resurrected, and spiritual death is overcome by all mankind being brought back into the presence of God. Thus, both the physical and spiritual deaths caused by Adam are automatically overcome by the Atonement of Christ.

However, there is more than overcoming the effects of the Fall of Adam that the Atonement must do if we desire to live with Heavenly Father forever. It can help us satisfy the law of God called justice and what it demands. Heavenly Father must be fair. He has given us commandments, and we are blessed if we keep them. However, for every broken commandment or law of God there must be a penalty or punishment. That's only fair! The person who breaks the commandment then owes justice. The more a person sins, the more he or she owes justice. Justice must be paid. Without the Atonement, whoever breaks a commandment must suffer for his or her own sins. Do you see the problem?

I have sinned, and so have you. Paul taught the Romans: "For all have sinned, and come short of the glory of God" (Romans 3:23). Therefore each of us is in debt to justice and must suffer until justice is satisfied. That doesn't sound like fun to me. Can you see that there must be a different way to pay justice? There is another way! Since Jesus never sinned—have you ever really thought about that statement?—he never owed justice anything. One who is perfect can therefore pay the price for the sins of others. That's what Christ did. No wonder the Apostle Paul wrote, "For ye are bought with a price" (1 Corinthians 6:20).

However, Christ requires something in return from us. He has said, "For behold, I, God, have suffered these things for all, that they might not suffer if they would repent; but if they would not repent they must suffer even as I" (D&C 19:16–17). Get the point? If I choose not to repent, then I suffer for my sins. If I repent, Jesus will suffer in my place. Which way do you want justice to be paid?

Another way of looking at justice is that it simply gives us what we deserve. That way God's justice is fair. Think for a minute, do we deserve the celestial kingdom? I don't think so. As a matter of fact, I know so.

You and I need more than what justice can give. Elder Dallin H. Oaks of the Quorum of the Twelve Apostles put it this way: "I cannot achieve my eternal goals on the basis of what I deserve. . . . To achieve my eternal goals, I need more than I deserve. I need more than justice" (*Sins, Crimes, and Atonement* [address delivered to Church Educational System, 7 February 1992], p. 2). Each of us needs mercy. Mercy is offered through the Atonement.

While the Atonement automatically overcomes the effects of the Fall of Adam and allows us back into the presence of God, our own sins can kick us out of His presence again. Notice Helaman 14:18: "Yea, and it [the Atonement] bringeth to pass the condition of repentance, that whosoever repenteth the same is not hewn down and cast into the fire; but whosoever repenteth not is hewn down and cast into the fire; and there cometh upon them again [and this time it's our own fault, not Adam's] a spiritual death, yea, a second death."

Why not let the Savior, who stands with open arms, pay the price in our place? That's one of the main reasons He came to earth.

Yet the Atonement must do more for us if we are to live with Heavenly Father forever. You see, it's one thing for the Atonement to pay the price of justice for our sins. It's another thing to take care of what sin does to us.

Let me try to explain. When we are born into the world, we are born innocent (see D&C 93:38). What are the odds that we'll sin after we reach the age of accountability? About one hundred percent. Each of us will sin again and again and cause our own spiritual death. It is through sin that one becomes a natural man. This natural man will continue to sin unless . . . and here is the key . . . "The natural man is an enemy to God, and has been from the fall of Adam, and will be, forever and ever, unless he yields to the enticings of the Holy Spirit, and putteth off the natural man and becometh a saint through the atonement of Christ the Lord" (Mosiah 3:19).

I need the Atonement to help me change! I need it to help me overcome those sins that I seem to just keep doing. We simply can't make this change on our own. As a bishop, I would see young people who would try so hard to overcome sins on their own, only to fall time and time again. Once they truly yielded to the Holy Ghost, they started their way back. As they did, the Atonement helped them become clean and worthy again. It helped them to change.

Listen to President Ezra Taft Benson, "The Lord works from the inside out. The world works from the outside in. . . . The world would mold men by changing their environment. Christ changes men, who then change their environment. The world would shape human behavior, but Christ can change human nature" ("Born of God," *Ensign*, November 1985, p. 6).

As Latter-day Saints, we must understand why we need the Savior. We need Him to overcome the effects of the Fall of Adam, to pay the demands of justice, and to help us change and become pure again. We cannot earn our way back to God. As Lehi taught his son Jacob, "There is no flesh that can dwell in the presence of God, save it be through the merits, and mercy, and grace of the Holy Messiah" (2 Nephi 2:8). Do you see the importance of the Atonement, that without it we all become like Lucifer and his angels? But with the Atonement, if we use it to its fullest, we have the potential to become like our Father in Heaven and His Son. One of my favorite hymns states:

> I marvel that he would descend from his throne divine
> To rescue a soul so rebellious and proud as mine,
> That he should extend his great love unto such as I,
> Sufficient to own, to redeem, and to justify.
>

Hymns [1985], no. 193

Let's live our lives so that others may see how much we love the Savior, how much we need the Savior, and how much we accept him as our Savior.

Curtis Jacobs has worked for the Church Educational System programs since 1979 and with the Especially for Youth program since 1984. He has taught seminary and institute in Arizona, and has spent the last few years teaching at Utah State University. He and his wife, Jolene, are the parents of four very active children. Curtis is a raquetball fanatic and loves Les Misérables.

Taking It Home

What's your favorite school subject? Math, English, history, physical education, art, music, computers—so many choices, so few electives. Sound familiar? My favorite class was woods. What a great class! Wood, machinery, and friends, what more would you need?

On the first day of wood shop, the teacher informed us that we couldn't go into the shop until we passed the tools test. For the next week we were introduced to each of the hand and power tools. Each of us had to convince the teacher that we were capable of using the tools and that we were not going to harm ourselves or those around us.

After we passed the test, the teacher told us that we had to learn to draw plans for our projects. He had decided that our first project would be a clipboard. I didn't really think that I needed a clipboard, but I consented to learn how to draw plans so I could make what I really wanted to make. The next week was spent copying plans off the board. We had to learn some architectural symbols and line qualities that represented the hidden views of our project. At length I convinced the teacher through my test and my drawing that I was ready to enter the shop. On the appropriate day I donned my shop glasses, gathered my materials, and started gluing my clipboard together. Eventually I got a B-plus on this project.

The teacher decided the next project also: a very disco nightstand. Again, I didn't really think that I needed a nightstand, but I consented to follow the plan so I could later make what I really wanted to make. Once again I copied the drawings off the board. My impatience for getting back to the shop really began to show. I think I got only a C on this set of drawings, but the teacher let me return to the shop anyway. Once again I gathered my materials, and I began cutting.

After gluing a face frame at the front of the nightstand, I discovered that it was about an eighth of an inch too big. Sheepishly I consulted the teacher. After examining my work, he suggested that I take a sixteenth of an inch off each side by using the table saw. I have to admit, the table saw scared me. The two-horsepower engine, ten-inch blade, and 240,000 revolutions per minute were intimidating. With fear and trepidation I measured and measured again. Then I flipped the switch, and the saw hummed to life with a haunting whirling sound. Carefully I started the face frame through. When I was halfway through the cut, another student from across the shop yelled, "I'll help you." I wasn't sure that I needed help, but he grabbed the opposite end anyway. Moments later he twisted the frame, the blade grabbed it, and the wood flew into my stomach.

The next thing I remember was lying on the ground with the class staring at me. Several murmured "Kickback" and "Are you all right?" The teacher soon came over. I was really trying to look all right while I was lying in agony and pain. I thought the teacher would come and help me. Instead he picked up the face frame, examined it closely, said, "I think it's still usable," and walked back to his project.

The next day he instructed me to turn over the frame so nobody could see the ugly gash left by the saw blade. This was only the first of a series of little and big mistakes. I finished the project sometime around Christmas. My mother acted surprised and pleased by the gift she had paid for me to make. Now, years later, the nightstand sits in my living room, mostly because our house is decorated in early-marriage style with pieces of furniture that others don't want. My mom gave the nightstand back when I moved out of the house. It's been with me ever since.

If you come to visit my house, I'll show you this wonderful piece of high-school industry. Today you would notice the Formica top. I still remember how we thought it was awesome. If you look closely, you'll see where I didn't really glue the Formica correctly. This might draw your attention to the front, where the doors with gargoyle handles don't really match because the face frame wasn't mounted square to the cabinet. Or perhaps you'll see the side of the cabinet that is lighter than the others because I was in a hurry to stain it before the cleanup bell. Maybe you would notice the trim that doesn't quite match because I didn't measure it accurately.

Every careless mistake I made in high-school wood shop is displayed now in my living room for every guest to see. The project I brought home in 1977 has followed me for more than twenty years. In a symbolic way, every careless mistake you make as a teenager will have a manifestation in your adult life. Even decisions that you think are insignificant will somehow haunt you later on. What kinds of things are you going to bring home with you? Let's talk about three significant choices you can make while you are still young: obeying the Word of Wisdom, staying morally clean, and preparing for the temple.

The Word of Wisdom

I don't think I have ever met a chain smoker, drug addict, or alcoholic who started out with the goal of being a slave to their appetites. Perhaps you have heard talks or presentations about people who were addicted but didn't mean to be. My experience has been that you never think that you will be addicted. For this reason, you might be convinced that the examples don't apply to you. Consider the following simple story:

Once there was a young man who had everything going for him. He was smart: he scored in the ninetieth percentile on the ACT. He was strong: he made the first-string, all state baseball, basketball, and track teams. He was popular: he was voted homecoming king and most likely to succeed by his senior class.

One night he and a friend decided to check in on a party one of their nonmember friends was having. They intended to stay for only a minute. When they heard the music and started talking with their friends, however, the party just got more exciting. Without really thinking, they both accepted a can of beer. What do you think happened?

A) The boy got in a car accident on the way home and ended up totaling the car, injuring his friend, suffering brain damage, and losing the use of one of his legs. His life was ruined: no college scholarship, no way to learn in school, and no car!

B) The police raided the party and found illegal drugs. Everyone was arrested, and the boy forfeited his college scholarship, everyone in the community found out, and his father took away his car!

C) The boy felt bad.

In the past you may have been convinced not to break the Word of Wisdom because you might lose your health, hurt someone, die, or lose your car. If these reasons work, that's great. These risks are real! However, some youth today have figured out that not everyone who drinks gets in accidents, not everyone who smokes dies of cancer, and not everyone who does drugs dies of an overdose. Instead there is a much more basic reason not to drink, smoke, or do drugs: you will feel bad! In reality, when you participate in these or any other addictive sin you will be separated from God (See Isaiah 59:1–3).

It may be difficult to understand, but I invite you to consider that when we break the Word of Wisdom the consequences include not only alcoholism, drug addiction, death, or loss of property but also separation from God. No wonder we may struggle to pray, read scriptures, attend church, or even be nice if our works have been sinful. Simply stated, you cannot break the Word of Wisdom and expect to love going to church, praying, or reading the scriptures. When you break the Word of Wisdom, what do you bring home? Whatever it is, it is not the Spirit.

Moral Cleanliness

My nightstand is adequate; it works as a place to store family pictures and games. As a piece of furniture, however, it is an embarrassment. Each of the little mistakes I made add up to make the nightstand less valuable. While I never intended for the nightstand to be ugly, today I realize that it is. Moral cleanliness is similar. You may never make one big mistake. Several smaller mistakes, however, may make you think that chastity and moral cleanliness are not important.

You have likely heard several talks on morality. Some of these talks may have centered on the effects of music, dress, and early dating on morality. Once again, it would be easy to misinterpret these messages by concluding that if you listen to immoral music, dress inappropriately, or date before you are sixteen you will eventually commit fornication. You probably know people who have proven that you can date before sixteen and not commit fornication. Consider the following story.

Once there was a young lady who was not very popular. She didn't have many friends, didn't really dress like everyone else, and struggled with most social situations. When her Young Women group began turning sixteen, all the girls began to date on the weekends. This heightened her loneliness. Not only didn't she get asked on dates, now her peers weren't even available to go to movies or have sleepovers on Friday nights.

During her senior year, this young lady met a boy who seemed genuinely interested. Once in a while he would say hi to her in the hallway. When homecoming came, he asked her to go. Since he was not that popular either, he didn't know anyone with whom he could double, so they went alone. After the dance they drove to her house, but instead of dropping her off he asked if she would like to drive up the canyon and look at the city lights. Hesitantly she agreed. At length she found herself involved in passionate kissing. Now you finish the story:

A) It was too late for her to stop. They continued in the passion of the moment, and before the night was over she was sure that she was in love. Within a month they decided not to date anyone else. By the end of her senior year, however, she was worried about how to care for a child instead of which college to attend.

B) It shocked her! After they were done kissing, they drove to her house. On the way the boy lost concentration, the car veered off the road, and both of them were killed before she ever had the opportunity to repent.

C) She felt bad.

What is the inevitable consequence of early dating? You lose the Spirit! Even if you don't French-kiss, get involved with petting, or commit fornication, what will you bring home? Whatever it is, it is not the Spirit. If you don't repent, not only do you risk moral uncleanliness but you risk loving darkness (see D&C 29:45).

Temple Preparation

Let's try a positive example. Perhaps you have had parents, leaders, and teachers who are attempting to get you to be more involved with the scriptures. Consider the following example.

Once there was a popular group of friends who just seemed to do everything together. Not only did they go to movies, study for tests, and hang out at each other's houses, but they also studied their scriptures. Seminary was their favorite class of the day. When their coaches tried to schedule practices during early-morning seminary, they bargained to stay later after school. When the swimming coach wouldn't bend, three of them decided to quit the swim team.

They promised each other that each evening before they did their homework or watched TV they would read their scriptures for thirty minutes. Sometimes they would call each other as a reminder. When one missed seminary, the others would copy their notes and share so they could all keep up. Now you finish the story.

A) Two of the young men went on missions and baptized the king of a far-off country. Subsequently the whole country opened to missionary work, and several dozen baptisms came from their initial efforts.
B) They all married in the temple and remain active leaders in their wards and stakes. One of the young women is a Relief Society president at only 23.
C) They all felt good.

Just as one cigarette will not guarantee that you get cancer and one immoral song will not ensure that you commit fornication, reading the scriptures will not guarantee successful missions, leadership positions, or temple marriages. In fact, the only sure result of scripture reading is that you will feel the Spirit. Make no mistake, however, about the importance of the scriptures. The likelihood of a successful mission, Church activity, moral cleanliness, and temple worthiness increases with scripture study. Alma explained this principle to Zeezrom: "He that will harden his heart, the same receiveth the lesser portion of the word; and he that will not harden his heart, to him is given the greater portion of the word, until it is given unto him to know the mysteries of God until he know them in full" (Alma 12:10).

Alma continues by explaining that those who have the lesser portion of the word will be led captive by the devil. Wow! In this case, all you have to do is receive a greater portion of the word and you will bring home the mysteries of God! If you receive a lesser portion, however, you will be captive.

What do you really want to bring home? As with my nightstand, it seems unfair that such minor choices can have such lasting consequences. Your home is likely a collection of items that are valuable to you, items that are necessary, items that are lost, and some junk. All of these things made it to your house because someone brought them in. The effort it took to find and keep these items is not always appropriate. A few of those possessions, however, are worth whatever effort it takes to ensure their safety and protection.

Upon completion of the clipboard and nightstand, the teacher let us build whatever we wanted. At the time, my mother was expecting my youngest brother. I knew that she wanted a baby bassinet. After looking at a few examples, I drew the plans, bought the wood, and began constructing the bassinet. I used all the skills I had mastered while making the clipboard and nightstand. While it was far from perfect, it worked for my brother.

Like the nightstand, the bassinet has followed me. Both of my children spent their first three months in my tenth-grade woods project. I am always amazed that something I did when I was so young has lasted for so long. Alma counseled his young son to "learn wisdom in thy youth; yea, learn in thy youth to keep the commandments of God" (Alma 37:35). What a great thing to bring home: the ability to keep the commandments. Consider the following comparison.

If you owned a delicate vase and were moving to a new home, how would you ensure that the vase would not be broken? Maybe you would buy a special box, pack it with those Styrofoam popcorn things, and mark the box with a big, red fragile sign on the outside. If this vase had been carried by your pioneer great-great-grand-mother across the plains, you may even insure the vase for several thousand dollars.

While it may be a stretch, imagine that your happiness and the happiness of your future children depended on that vase staying intact. In that case, you may not trust a mover to take care of the vase. You would likely take care of the vase yourself. You would pack it yourself, carry it yourself, unpack it yourself, and even place it yourself. Most likely you would feel a little bit safer when the vase was in place. You would watch, dust, and care for the vase after it was in your new home.

Caring for your personal testimony is similar to caring for an heirloom. You must anticipate potential dangers. Your testimony may be endangered by the Internet, immoral music, steady dating, anger, hatred, cheating on tests, or experimenting with drugs or alcohol. Like the vase, your testimony is extremely valuable, even irreplaceable. Mosiah 4:30 suggests that we need to watch ourselves, our thoughts, words, and deeds and that we also need to "observe the commandments of God, and continue in the faith of what ye have heard concerning the coming of our Lord." Take care of that testimony.

In a coming day, I know that you and I will appear before the Lord to be judged. What do we suppose we will have brought with us? As you finish this chapter, consider some of the tremendous treasures we could bring home to the Lord when this life is over:

1. "Works of righteousness upon the face of the earth" (Alma 5:16).
2. Knowledge that Christ is the "true light" (see D&C 93:1–2).
3. Our eternal families (see D&C 130:2; 131:2).
4. Experience for our good (see D&C 122:7).

I know that the Holy Ghost is a delicate possession. Immoral music, disregard for the words of the prophet, neglect of the scriptures, unkind words, not honoring our parents, or even forgetting to pray can cause the Spirit to leave. Without that Spirit we can't make it home from sacrament meeting with any noticeable change, much less return to our Heavenly Father after having fulfilled our purposes for coming to earth. Whatever measures are necessary to protect your worthiness are worth the effort. Only through righteousness can you hope to return to Heavenly Father with the precious gifts He intended you to receive.

Kim M. Peterson is a seminary coordinator and institute instructor in the Denver, Colorado, area. He loves to ski and has been employed as a ski instructor during the winter months. Kim also enjoys cooking a variety of Eastern dishes. He and his wife, Terri, have one son and one daughter.

A SEASON FOR COURAGE
ESPECIALLY FOR YOUTH 1999 SONGBOOK

Anyone can enjoy playing and singing the songs from this summer's EFY programs at Brigham Young University. The theme "A Season for Courage" permeates each song in the songbook. Such LDS songwriters as Merrill Jenson, Tyler Castleton, Staci Peters, Cherie Call, Greg Simpson, and Julie de Azevedo express thoughts of faith, hope, and courage in these pieces.

Song titles include "A Season for Courage," "Fearless Heart," "When All Is Said and Done," "Promises I Keep," "Feel the Fire," and "The Watchmen." Appropriate for use at home, at seminary devotionals, or at special Church-related events. Includes lyrics and piano accompaniment.

3851858 $10.95
ISBN 1-57345-559-8